FIREFLY
The Big Damn Cookbook

ISBN: 9781789092417

Published by Titan Books
A division of Titan Publishing Group Ltd.
144 Southwark St.
London
SE1 0UP

First edition: 2019
1 3 5 7 9 10 8 6 4 2

Based on the series created by Joss Whedon

Did you enjoy this book? We love to hear from our readers.
Please e-mail us at: readerfeedback@titanemail.com or write to Reader
Feedback at the above address.

To receive advance information, news, competitions, and exclusive offers online,
please sign up for the Titan newsletter on our website: www.titanbooks.com

A CIP catalogue record for this title is available from the British Library.

Printed and bound in China.

firefly

THE BIG DAMN COOKBOOK

To Malika,
Keep flying through the kitchen!

Chelsea Monroe-Cassel

TITAN BOOKS

CONTENTS

KAYLEE'S NOTE

So, I thought it'd be real nice if everybody on the ship could share their favorite recipes. I'll put 'em into a big book, and we can keep it in the kitchen for when we make food together. Sometimes it's nice to have a real meal, you know? We're like a family, so a family cookbook would be just shiny.

Kaylee

INTRODUCTION

FOOD IN THE 'VERSE

Settlers have to make do with whatever the 'Verse throws at them, including bad harvests and seemingly interminable winters. Often dropped with nothing more than what they could pack into a wagon, they survive by ingenuity and sheer force of will out there on some of them planets what's far from the Alliance's mind.

Terraforming has destroyed much of whatever native plants might have once grown on the Border planets, leaving the settlers there reliant on the Alliance shipments of Gen-seed and rations. But the odd smuggler travels through those systems, too, bringing a wider variety of seedlings and plants. There's even a rumor of a fellow who travels planet to planet, quietly seeding them with fruit trees like some sort of Earth-That-Was hero.

But in general, if you ain't living on one of the wealthy central planets, you'll make your peace with a lot of preserved, canned, and dried ingredients suited to travel. Soups and sauces, for example, usually come in powdered packets, and are mixed up as needed with a little boiled water. These recipes that follow are the from-scratch versions of those common elements.

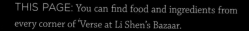

THIS PAGE: You can find food and ingredients from every corner of 'Verse at Li Shen's Bazaar.

FLOURS – The central planets have every type of flour that money can buy available to them. Nut flours are especially popular, partly because they are labor-intensive to grow, a clear indicator of wealth. Most folks make do with ordinary wheat flour, although you'll find some buckwheat and rye here and there, depending on what seeds got sent with the last shipment of Gen-seed.

BUTTER – Settlers on the Outer Rim and most of the Border planets prefer to use salted butter, as it keeps longer than unsalted. Some what dwell on the Core worlds, though, turn their noses up at that, and like their butter unsalted and fresh as can be. Seems silly to me. A little salt makes everything taste better!

SEASONINGS – Salt, pepper, ginger, garlic, and soy sauce make up a lot of the flavors you'll see out here. Five-spice is maybe the most common seasoning, used by everybody from one end of the 'Verse to the other. Made outta spices that would have been expensive back on Earth-That-Was, you can hardly find a kitchen out here that doesn't have a bottle of the stuff. It's good on meats, desserts, drinks, and all manner of other recipes, which I suppose is why it's so popular. Everybody has their own blend, seems like. If you're feelin' fancy, you can grind your own from whole spices. I've included a recipe for my favorite mix in the Basics section of this book on page 19.

SWEETENERS – Honey has to be one of the most amazing ingredients in the 'Verse. It might be mighty expensive on the central planets, but on the Border worlds, where it's harvested, most folks that have a mind to keep bees can and do. Soon as a planet's been terraformed, the bees pretty well make their own way, provided there're enough flowering things. Apart from honey, crops of sugar beets and sugar cane are grown pretty widely. They're bigger crops, so the sugar's cheaper for them's that need it.

PROTEIN – Comes in all colors of the rainbow, but believe me when I tell you that some of the cheaper varieties have a decidedly unlovely flavor. Best to avoid those and go for the mid-range stuff, if you can. Sources are all different: whey from the dairy farms, a variety of plant stuffs, and a whole slew of lab-grown types. Might not be 'specially appealing at times, but they'll keep a man going when he ain't got nothing else.

MEATS – Figure if you can shoot it, you can probably cook and eat it. Ain't no alien life in the 'Verse, so anything runnin' around on a planet was brought from Earth-That-Was. Cattle and chickens are pretty popular, and so are goats and pigs, since they'll eat near anything. Even seen horse and dog on some menus. I've heard rumors about some pretty strange hybrid meats in the Core, but can't swear to it.

SHINDIGS

Food ain't just for keeping your belly full. It's also for celebratin'! Can be hard to keep track of days and dates out in the Black, on account of there bein' no single sun, but sometimes you remember it's someone's birthday, or weddin' anniversary, or sometimes you just want to do somethin' special for those that you love. Or sometimes you pull off a job with a minimum of hiccups, and Cap'n declares it's worth commemoratin'. I put together some of my favorite menus for different occasions here. Makes plannin' a shindig a lot easier, with less arguin' over the details.

Note: Cap'n wants to remind everyone that guns and plastic dinosaurs are not allowed at the dinner table.

FAMILY CELEBRATIONS

Besides birthdays, marriages, and funerals, celebrations outside the Core are as diverse as the folks celebratin'. Some planets throw a party for the harvest, or to remember somethin' important. Some folks still celebrate festivals from Earth-That-Was. Most everyone cooks fillin', hearty meals usin' the ingredients they've got on hand — it's all about bein' together with family and friends, not about impressin' the neighbors.

When we get supplies in, the Serenity likes to get together to have a proper sit-down family meal. Rule is the cook never cleans, unless they got real bad luck at chore poker.

STARTER
Wife Soup
Tear & Share Rolls

MAIN
Chicken & Dumplings
Garlic Green Beans
Fresh Tomato Slices
Mashed Sesame Spuds

DESSERT
Chocolate Protein Cake

FORMAL PARTIES

The Alliance Brass like throwin' events for any old thing — new buildings, award ceremonies, pattin' themselves on the backs for bein' masters of the 'Verse. It's hard to imagine throwin' that kind of money around while other folks out there are starvin'; on the other hand, it's a good excuse to wear a pretty dress.

We never had occasion to host a real extravagant 'do on Serenity, but I took notes on the spread at the party we attended on Persephone. Everything looked so fancy! Never found out what that hot cheese thing was, though.

CANAPÉS
Stuffed Mushrooms
Sweet Potato Bites
Tofu Cubes
Crab Dip
Spiced Tea Eggs
Badger's Finger Sandwiches
Lotus Chips

COCKTAILS
Gunpowder Gimlet
Sake Cocktail
Frye Fizzler
Shimmerwine

THE BASICS

WHITE SAUCE, 18
BROWN SAUCE, 18
SWEET CHILI SAUCE, 19
FIVE-SPICE MIX, 19
DOUGH FOR BAO, 20
PASTRY DOUGH, 20
BISCUITS, 23

Nothing spruces up ordinary protein packs like a good sauce. These are adaptable and can be tweaked pretty easy for whatever you have in the galley.

WHITE SAUCE

Prep: 5 minutes
Makes: 1 batch
Dietary: Veg, Vegan*
Classification: Basics
Difficulty: Easy

INGREDIENTS

2 Tbsp butter
2 Tbsp flour
Pinch of salt and pepper
1 cup milk, warm

METHOD

In a small saucepan, melt the butter over medium heat. Whisk in the flour, salt, and pepper and let cook for about a minute, until starting to turn golden. Gradually whisk in the milk, then continue to cook for another minute or two, until thickened and smooth. Use straight away, or chill until ready to use.

VARIATIONS

Cheesy: Stir in ½–1 cup shredded cheese to the mixture once it's done but still hot. Great over vegetables.

Herbaceous: Stir in ½ tsp dried herbs or 1 tsp fresh herbs, if you can come by them. Real good on fish or chicken.

USED IN

Chicken & Dumplings

BROWN SAUCE

Prep: 5 minutes
Makes: 1 batch
Dietary: GF, Veg*, Vegan*
Classification: Basics
Difficulty: Easy

INGREDIENTS

2 Tbsp sesame oil
1 Tbsp minced garlic
1 Tbsp minced ginger
¼ cup soy sauce
½ cup chicken broth
2 Tbsp rice wine
2 Tbsp brown sugar
2 Tbsp cornstarch
½ cup water

METHOD

Heat the sesame oil in a medium frying pan over medium heat. Cook the garlic and ginger for a minute or two, until soft and fragrant. Add the soy sauce, chicken broth, rice wine, and brown sugar, and cook for another minute or two, until the sugar has been dissolved.

In a small separate bowl, combine the cornstarch and the water, stirring until the cornstarch has completely dissolved into a slurry. Pour this into the pan with the other ingredients and bring up to a boil. The sauce should thicken considerably as it cooks.

USE AS A DIPPING SAUCE FOR

Sausage Rolls
Shadow Spare Ribs
Street Chicken Skewers

螢火蟲

SWEET CHILI SAUCE

Prep: 10 minutes
Makes: 1 batch
Dietary: GF, Veg, Vegan
Classification: Basics
Difficulty: Easy

INGREDIENTS

½ cup rice vinegar
½ cup granulated sugar
½ cup water
2 Tbsp Shaoxing wine
2 tsp red pepper flakes
6 cloves garlic, minced
1–2 inches ginger, grated
2 tsp cornstarch
1 Tbsp soy sauce

METHOD

Combine all the ingredients except the cornstarch and soy sauce in a small saucepan. Place over medium heat and bring up to a simmer, then cook for around 5 minutes until the sugar has dissolved and the flavors have melded together. In a small bowl, combine the cornstarch and soy sauce. Stir the cornstarch mixture into the main pot and cook the sauce for another minute or so, until it has thickened somewhat. Transfer to a bowl or serving container and let cool completely. Adjust to taste, if needed. Store in the fridge for around a week.

USE AS A DIPPING SAUCE FOR

Corn Dodgers
Fresh Bao
Garlic Green Beans
Roast Duck
Sausage Rolls
Shadow Spare Ribs
Street Chicken Skewers

FIVE-SPICE MIX

Prep: 5 minutes
Makes: 1 batch
Dietary: GF, Veg, Vegan
Classification: Basics
Difficulty: Easy

INGREDIENTS

2 tsp Sichuan or black peppercorns
5 star anise seeds
½ tsp ground cloves
1 tsp cinnamon
1 Tbsp fennel seeds

METHOD

Toast the peppercorns in a hot skillet for 1–2 minutes, until aromatic. Put all ingredients in a spice grinder or coffee grinder and process to a fine powder. Keep fresh in an airtight container stored in a cool, dark place.

USED IN

Canned Peach Cobbler
Five-spice Caramel
Pork & Beans
Pork Jerky
Saffron Rice Pudding
Spiced Plum Fruit Leather
Steamed Pumpkin Buns
Street Chicken Skewers

螢火蟲

DOUGH FOR BAO

Prep: 10 minutes   Rising: 1 hour
Makes: 1 batch
Dietary: Veg, Vegan
Classification: Basics
Difficulty: Middling

INGREDIENTS

¾ cup warm water
2 Tbsp granulated sugar
Pinch of salt
2 tsp instant dry yeast
2¼ cups flour
2 Tbsp cornstarch
1 Tbsp vegetable oil

METHOD

In a small bowl, combine the water, sugar, salt, and yeast. In a separate bowl, stir together the flour and cornstarch. Add to this the yeast mixture, stirring to combine everything evenly. When the dough has come together, tip it on a clean, lightly floured work surface and knead for several minutes until soft and smooth, but not sticky. Brush the dough with oil so it doesn't stick to anything when it rises, place the dough ball back into the bowl, and cover lightly with plastic. Set somewhere warm to rise for at least an hour, or until doubled in size.

USED IN

Fresh Bao
Sausage Rolls
Steamed Pumpkin Buns *(For this recipe, substitute 5 oz pumpkin puree for ¼ cup of the water.)*

PASTRY DOUGH

Prep: 5 minutes   Chilling: 30 minutes
Makes: 1 single crust batch of dough
Dietary: Veg*, Vegan*
Classification: Basics
Difficulty: Easy

INGREDIENTS

1¼ cups all-purpose flour
¼ tsp salt
3 Tbsp butter, chilled
3 Tbsp lard
¼ cup ice water

METHOD

Combine the flour and salt in a medium mixing bowl. Using a pastry blender or a pair of knives, cut in the butter and lard until you have fairly small pieces of fat mixed evenly through. Drizzle in a little of the water and toss the dough with a fork to mix, adding a little water at a time until the dough comes together. Form the dough into a flat disc, wrap in plastic, and chill for at least 30 minutes.

USED IN

Mama Reynolds' Shoofly Pie
Meat Pies

螢火蟲

BISCUITS

Prep: 10 minutes   Baking: 15 minutes
Makes: 1 batch
Dietary: Veg, Vegan*
Classification: Basics
Difficulty: Easy

INGREDIENTS

3 cups flour
2 Tbsp baking powder
1 tsp salt
¾ cup butter, cold and cubed
1 cup buttermilk

METHOD

In a medium mixing bowl, stir together the dry ingredients. Cut the butter into the flour with a pastry cutter or a pair of butter knives until the mixture's all crumbly looking. Stir in the buttermilk, but only until just combined. Dump the dough out onto your work surface and flatten it into a large disc about 1 inch thick. Cut into round shapes about 3 inches wide, then reform the dough and do it again until everything is used up. Put the biscuits on the baking sheet and bake for about 15 minutes, until golden on top.

This recipe makes a great side on its own.

USED IN

Chicken & Dumplings
Strawberry Shortcake (*Add ¼ cup*
brown sugar to dough. Before baking, brush
them with a little heavy cream and sprinkle
with extra brown sugar.)

螢火蟲

RECIPES FOR SHIPBOARD LIVING

SIMON'S
DRIED SPIRO-BALLS
10 BALLS

The Core has a give and take relationship with the Border planets, where the farmers mostly give, and the Alliance mostly takes. With one notable exception: some of the Border planets have also adopted algae farms, though none are as extensive as those below the Sea of Bellerophon. Those farms export superfood algae to some of the Border worlds in powder form, or to the other Core worlds as these little bite-sized energy balls.

TIME
Prep: 15 minutes
Chill: 15 minutes

COURSE
Snack

DIETARY
GF, Veg, Vegan

DIFFICULTY
Middling

INGREDIENTS	METHOD

5 pitted dates
½ cup sunflower seeds
½ cup raw pumpkin seeds
1 Tbsp coconut oil
1 Tbsp nut butter
2 tsp spirulina
½ tsp cinnamon
2 Tbsp chia seeds

Combine the dates and seeds in a food processor and pulse until you have a fine, crumbly consistency. Add the coconut oil, then just enough nut butter to bring the mixture together into a consistency that mostly holds its shape. Stir in the remaining ingredients and form into 10 balls. Chill for at least 15 minutes, or until ready to eat.

螢火蟲

ZOE'S
SHIPBOARD CRACKERS
24 - 36 CRACKERS

They might not look like much, but they'll keep you going when there's not much else on board. On Earth-That-Was, sailors used to bake up batches of something similar and let it dry. Hardtack, they called it, and this ain't far off. Not too bad with a little cheese, if you ain't run out of that yet.

TIME
Prep: 15 minutes
Cook: 15 minutes

COURSE
Snack

DIETARY
Veg, Vegan

DIFFICULTY
Easy

INGREDIENTS

15 oz can garbanzo beans
3 cloves garlic, minced
¼ cup olive oil, plus more for top
1½ cups flour
3 Tbsp nutritional yeast
1 tsp sugar
½ tsp salt,
        plus more for sprinkling
Up to ¼ cup water
Assorted seeds, such as sesame,
        poppy, or chia, for topping

METHOD

Preheat the oven to 450°F and set out a baking sheet.

Puree the garbanzo beans and their liquid in a food processor along with the garlic and olive oil until you have a nice smooth paste. Transfer it to a bowl, then add the flour, yeast, sugar, and salt. Gradually mix in just enough water to make a soft dough, then let it rest for around 10 minutes.

Roll the dough out flat on the baking sheet, to about ¼ inch thickness. Poke it all over with the tines of a fork, then brush with extra olive oil. Sprinkle with salt and your choice of toppings, then slice into small pieces. Bake for 15 minutes, or until turning golden on the edges.

ZOE'S
SPICED PLUM
FRUIT LEATHER

8 - 10 ROLLS

I grew utterly tired of the rations we had during the war, but there's no denying the convenience and occasional need for a quick bite that restores your energy. During one of our jobs, I met a woman making these out on one of the Border worlds to preserve some of her season's fruit crops just before the Alliance came to collect their cut. Just so happens I forget to tell them what I saw, and she shared the recipe with me as thanks. A lot of packaged foodstuffs leave a lot to be desired, so I like to fix up my own from time to time.

TIME
Prep: 20 minutes
Cook: 3+ hours

COURSE
Snack

DIETARY
GF, Veg, Vegan

DIFFICULTY
Easy

INGREDIENTS

2 cups plums, washed,
        pitted, and diced
2 cups apple, washed, cored,
        and diced
½ cup water or apple juice
½ tsp five-spice

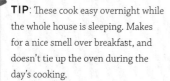

TIP: These cook easy overnight while the whole house is sleeping. Makes for a nice smell over breakfast, and doesn't tie up the oven during the day's cooking.

METHOD

Preheat the oven to 180°F and line a good sized baking sheet with parchment paper.

Combine all the ingredients in a medium saucepan and cook over medium heat for around 15 minutes, until the fruit is very soft. Mash the fruit and spread out on the prepared baking sheet. To start, bake for 3 hours on low heat. Then check every 20 minutes or so, pulling the fruit leather from the oven when the mixture is dried out and no longer sticky to the touch. Let the leather cool and then cut into long strips, paper and all. Coil these and store in an airtight container.

螢火蟲

FRESH TOMATO SLICES

2 - 4 SERVINGS

When you have real, fresh produce that came from a garden, not a can, it's best to let the edibles speak for themselves rather than messing with some overly complex recipe. This one's so good, you can practically taste the dirt on it, and I mean that in the best way.

TIME
Prep: 5 minutes

COURSE
Snack

DIETARY
GF, Veg, Vegan

DIFFICULTY
Easy

INGREDIENTS

2 large tomatoes
1 clove garlic, minced
1 tsp sesame oil
1 Tbsp rice vinegar
1 Tbsp soy sauce
½ tsp salt
1 pinch ground pepper

METHOD

Cut the tomatoes into slices ¼ inch–½ inch thick, and arrange on a plate. Combine the remaining ingredients in a small bowl and drizzle over the top of the tomatoes.

WASH'S
CRUNCHY SNACK MIX
MAKES ENOUGH FOR A SINGLE LONG VOYAGE

I'm a snacker. I'll admit it. There are some mighty exciting moments in a pilot's life. But there are also mighty long, dull periods of not doing much of anything but staring into the black. It's so boring, with the dark and the going and the lack of steering. For those times, there are snacks. I first encountered something like this in a bar on Persephone, but my version is better.

TIME
Prep: 5 minutes
Cook: 1 hour

COURSE
Snack

DIETARY
GF*, Veg, Vegan*

DIFFICULTY
Easy

INGREDIENTS

5 cups mixed rice and corn cereals
2 cups thin pretzels
1 cup sesame sticks
¾ cup wasabi peas
½ cup whole almonds
4 Tbsp melted butter
2 Tbsp sesame oil
2 Tbsp brown sugar
2 Tbsp soy sauce
1 tsp garlic powder
½ tsp onion powder
⅛ tsp ground cumin
½ tsp cayenne pepper

METHOD

Preheat the oven to 225°F and line a baking sheet with parchment paper.

In a large mixing bowl, combine all the dry ingredients. In a separate small bowl, combine the butter, oil, sugar, soy sauce, and seasonings. Drizzle this over the dry mix and toss to coat evenly. Transfer the snack mix to the baking sheet and bake for about an hour, stirring once in a while. Let cool for about 15 minutes before eating.

TIP: To make it last even longer, eat it with chopsticks. Did I mention piloting can be boring?

螢火蟲

JAYNE'S

PORK JERKY

10 - 12 PIECES

Now *these* are a real good snack for when you're on a job, stuck on a hillside waitin' on spoilin' an ambush or the like. I usually get 'em when we're planet-side, but if I gotta make 'em myself, I do.

TIME
Marinate: 8 hours
Cook: 40 minutes

COURSE
Snack

DIETARY
GF

DIFFICULTY
Easy

INGREDIENTS

1 lb ground pork
¾ cup sugar
1 Tbsp soy sauce
1 tsp salt
½ tsp five-spice

TIP: If you want to make 'em fancier, brush with a little honey and put some sesame seeds on top, but that ain't needed.

METHOD

Combine the ingredients in a medium mixing bowl and mix 'em up. Cover and let it sit overnight in the fridge so the flavors go all through the meat.

Heat the oven to 250°F and fit a piece of parchment paper to a big baking sheet. Spread the pork mix over that, pressing it real thin, maybe about ¼ inch thick. Bake it for 15 minutes, then flip the whole mess over. Bake for another 15 minutes, then take it outta the oven. Cut it into some squares, whatever size fits best in your pack. Put a couple pieces at a time back on the baking sheet, then broil 'em for a minute or so, not too close to the heat, until they're a good dark color. Flip and do it again, maybe half the time.

Store in an airtight container, and keep cool if you ain't going to eat 'em right off.

螢火蟲

螢火蟲

IT'S GOOD. IT TASTES LIKE...
IT'S GOOD.

Simon

SIMON'S

EGGY OAT MUSH

1 - 2 SERVINGS

I'm admittedly not much of a deft hand in the kitchen, but I think I'm getting better. This savory breakfast... mush... certainly isn't as bad as the first time I made it. Even River will occasionally eat some now. It's a wholesome start to the day, even if most of the ingredients on the ship are canned or dried, rather than fresh.

TIME

Cook: 15 minutes

COURSE

Savory

DIETARY

GF, Veg

DIFFICULTY

Easy

INGREDIENTS	METHOD

1 Tbsp butter
½–1 cup mixed vegetables, minced
1 clove garlic, minced
1 cup vegetable or chicken broth
½ cup rolled oats
Splash of milk
1 egg, beaten
Salt and pepper, to taste

Melt the butter in a large frying pan, then add the vegetables and garlic. Cook for around 5 minutes, then add the broth and oats. Cook for another 5 minutes or so, until the oats are soft. Add the splash of milk and bring back up to a simmer. Remove from heat and add the egg, stirring for a couple of minutes until it's completely cooked and mixed in evenly. Season to taste with salt and pepper. I also like some spicy pepper flakes in mine, but River makes a face if I add them to hers.

BOOK'S

SHEPHERD
CHICKEN SOUP

4 SERVINGS

Sometimes the simplest things can surprise you. For me, a moment of revelation came with a bowl of simple, honest soup, and I feel I've been on the right path ever since. I'm sure this recipe is far richer than the version I partook of in that homeless shelter, but the principle is the same: good, wholesome ingredients combined to make a nourishing broth full of the richness of life.

螢火蟲

TIME
Prep: 5 minutes
Cook: 1½ hours

COURSE
Savory

DIETARY
GF*

DIFFICULTY
Middling

INGREDIENTS

1 Tbsp butter

½ onion, diced

1 leek, white and pale green parts
        sliced thin

1 carrot, chopped

2 stalks celery, chopped

1 Tbsp ginger, minced

2 cloves garlic, minced

½ tsp ground turmeric

½ tsp marjoram

2 cups chicken stock

3 cups water

2 large chicken thighs, boneless and
        skinless

1 cup pearl couscous

Salt and pepper, to taste

Fresh parsley, to garnish

METHOD

In a medium saucepan, melt the butter over medium heat. Add the onion, leek, carrot, and celery, and cook for about 5 minutes, until soft. Add the ginger, garlic, turmeric, and marjoram, and cook for another minute, until fragrant. Add the stock, water, and chicken thighs, then cover and set to a low simmer for about an hour, when the chicken should be cooked through. Scoop out the chicken and place in a bowl to cool. Add the couscous to the pot and simmer for 15 minutes, until the couscous is cooked through. While the couscous is cooking, shred the meat into bite-sized pieces. When the couscous is soft and puffed up, add the chicken back into the pot. Season to taste with salt and pepper, and sprinkle with a little parsley to garnish.

TIP: For a richer version, add a splash of heavy cream just before serving.

螢火蟲

TEAR & SHARE ROLLS

16 ROLLS

This here's a great recipe for when you've got a lot of mouths to feed. It's got to rise a while, but other than that it's pretty quick. I can only make it when we've recently restocked the kitchen at some outpost, on account of the flour and butter it uses, but everybody seems to like 'em, so I figure they're worth the trouble.

TIME
Prep: 10 minutes
Rise: 1½ hours
Bake: 25 minutes

COURSE
Savory

DIETARY
Veg

DIFFICULTY
Middling

INGREDIENTS

STARTER

2 Tbsp flour
¼ cup sweetened condensed milk
¼ cup water

DOUGH

3 cups flour
2 tsp instant dry yeast
1 tsp salt
¼ cup sweetened condensed milk
1 egg
½ cup water
2 Tbsp butter, softened,
        plus more for brushing

METHOD

Make the starter by whisking together the flour, condensed milk, and water in a frying pan over medium heat for around 5 minutes, until thickened but not lumpy. Remove from heat and let cool.

In a large mixing bowl, combine the flour, yeast, and salt, then make a well in the center and add the rest of the condensed milk and the egg. Mix in the starter, then begin adding water until the dough just comes together. Turn out onto a lightly floured work surface and begin to knead. After a minute or so, knead in the butter until fully incorporated and the dough bounces back when poked. Cover and let rise for roughly and hour, until doubled in size.

Once the dough is done rising, split into 16 equal pieces. Flatten each piece of dough into a long strip, then roll it up lengthwise. Set 'em all in a lightly buttered 8 x 8 inch baking pan, alternating the rolls facing clockwise and anti-clockwise. Turn on your oven to 350°F and let 'em rise again for half an hour, until puffed up again. Brush the tops with some melted butter, then bake for about 25 minutes, until they're golden brown on top. If you've got the butter to spare, brush 'em again while they're still hot.

KAYLEE'S

FAMILY SOUP

4 SERVINGS

We used to eat this all the time when I was growin' up, on account of how flexible it is. My pa used to put all sorts of canned vegetables, roots, beans, and plenty of other stuff in the pot, but you let anything cook long enough, and add some seasoning, and it's bound to turn out pretty tasty. Celery, parsnips, corn, peppers, potatoes, barley... you name it, it went into a pot at some point! It's also a great way to use up any, uh... mismatched canned goods you might have on hand.

TIME	**COURSE**	**DIETARY**	**DIFFICULTY**
Prep: 15 minutes	Savory	GF	Easy
Cook: 25+ minutes			

INGREDIENTS

1 Tbsp vegetable oil
½ onion, diced
2–3 cloves garlic, minced
½ lb lean ground beef
1 cup chicken broth
28 oz can diced tomatoes
15 oz can kidney beans, rinsed
15 oz can mixed vegetables, drained
½ tsp dried savory, or other herbs
½ tsp cumin
Salt and pepper, to taste

METHOD

Heat the vegetable oil in the bottom of a large saucepan over medium heat, then brown the onion and garlic, then the beef, for about 5 minutes. Add the remaining ingredients and bring up to a low simmer. Let cook for at least 20 minutes, or longer if you've got time.

Goes great with garlic bread or the rolls on page 40. It's also real good with some hot Chinese pepper, if you can come by it, but ordinary red pepper flakes'll do just fine.

螢火蟲

Cheesy Grits

THE NEXT TIME YOUR FAMILY
COMES TOGETHER AROUND THE
DINNER TABLE, MAKE SURE
THEY HAVE A HEARTY HELPING
OF GRITS! SOME LIKE THEM
WITH GREENS, SOME LIKE THEM
WITH CHEESE, BUT ONE THING
EVERYONE CAN AGREE ON:
BLUE SUN GRITS ARE THE BEST
IN THE 'VERSE!

Tip: This dish is easy to dress up by adding sausage, cooked bacon, spicy peppers, or other meats and vegetables of your choice

MAKES 2–4 SERVINGS

PREP: 5 MINUTES
BAKING: 1 HOUR

DIETARY: GF, VEG
CLASSIFICATION: SAVORY
DIFFICULTY: EASY

INGREDIENTS:
2 CUPS WATER
½ TSP SALT
½ CUP BLUE SUN
   QUICK-COOKING GRITS
1 CUP BLUE SUN SHREDDED
   CHEDDAR CHEESE
½ CUP BLUE SUN WHOLE
   KERNEL CORN
1 TBSP BLUE SUN BUTTER
1 EGG, BEATEN

Preheat the oven to 350°F and lightly butter a small casserole dish.

Add the water and salt to a small saucepan and bring to a boil over medium-high heat. Stir in the grits and reduce heat to medium-low, then cook for around 5 minutes. Remove from heat and beat in the cheese, whole corn, butter, and the egg. Transfer everything to the casserole dish and bake for around an hour, until puffy and golden brown on top.

WIFE SOUP

2 - 4 SERVINGS

Zoe made this for me when we were first married. I don't know if it has another name, but I've always called it "Wife Soup" and, even though it's full of vegetables, I really like it. We don't usually have all the ingredients for it on the ship, so when she makes a bowl, I know I must have been good.

TIME
Prep: 5 minutes
Cook: 30 minutes

COURSE
Savory

DIETARY
GF, Veg, Vegan*

DIFFICULTY
Middling

INGREDIENTS

1 leek, sliced in half
        lengthwise
1 potato, cubed
3 cloves garlic
2 Tbsp olive oil
3 cups vegetable broth
2 Tbsp white miso
1 Tbsp rice vinegar
1 cup peas
3 Tbsp heavy cream
Zaatar, to garnish

METHOD

Preheat the oven to 400°F and line a baking sheet with parchment paper. Toss all the vegetables (except the peas) and garlic cloves with olive oil and spread out on the baking sheet. Roast for around 20 minutes, until all the vegetables are soft but not too browned.

Add the broth, miso, and rice vinegar to a medium saucepan over medium heat and stir until the miso is dissolved. Add in the roasted vegetables and cook for another minute or so. Add the peas, cook for a further minute, then puree everything in an upright blender or with an immersion blender. Immediately pour into serving bowls, garnish with cream and zaatar, and serve.

It's great with some crusty garlic bread.

螢火蟲

WASH'S
MASHED SESAME SPUDS
4 SERVINGS

Zoe taught me how to make this dish. It's no-nonsense, just like her. I mean, have you seen her mad? Really mad? It's a terrifying thing. Which is why I'm happy to make dinner. AND do the dishes. Very, very happy…

TIME
Prep: 5 minutes
Cook: 15 minutes

COURSE
Savory

DIETARY
GF, Veg, Vegan*

DIFFICULTY
Easy

INGREDIENTS	METHOD

2 lb russet potatoes, washed and cut into chunks
4-6 Tbsp butter, softened
½ cup heavy cream
1 tsp sesame oil, plus more to drizzle
Salt and pepper, to taste
Sesame seeds, to garnish

Bring a large pot half filled with water to a boil, then add the potatoes. Cook for around 15 minutes, or until the potatoes are tender. Drain the potatoes and transfer to a large bowl.

Add the butter and heavy cream, then start mashing. You want a pretty smooth consistency, so tweak the amounts of butter and cream if needed. Stir in the sesame oil, then season to taste with salt and pepper. Transfer to a serving bowl and drizzle with a little extra sesame oil and the sesame seeds to garnish.

螢火蟲

BOOK'S

SOUTHDOWN ABBEY COUSCOUS

WITH ROASTED VEGETABLES
4 SERVINGS

I learned to make this dish during my stay at the Southdown Abbey and, since everyone on Serenity so enjoyed it when I made it for them, it seemed a natural choice for this collection. At the abbey, we were encouraged to think of our small place amongst the greatness of the world, and to celebrate life. For me, the best way to do that was tending the abbey gardens. It can be difficult to come by fresh vegetables while traveling, though, so use whatever is available to you.

TIME
Prep: 5 minutes
Cook: 30 minutes

COURSE
Savory

DIETARY
Veg, Vegan*

DIFFICULTY
Middling

INGREDIENTS

2 parsnips, diced large
3 carrots, diced large
1 small red onion, chopped
8 oz brussels sprouts, halved
4 cloves garlic, minced
¼ cup olive oil, plus 2 Tbsp more
1 cup pearl couscous
1¼ cups water
2 tsp honey, warm
1 Tbsp rice vinegar
1 Tbsp soy sauce
Salt and pepper, to taste

METHOD

Preheat your oven to 350°F and set out a large baking sheet.

Toss the vegetables with the olive oil and minced garlic until they are all coated, then transfer them to the baking sheet. Cover loosely with foil and bake for 30 minutes, then uncover and bake for another 15, until slightly browned and tender.

While the vegetables are roasting, make the couscous by bringing the water and 1 Tbsp olive oil to a boil in a small saucepan. Add the couscous and turn the heat to low. Cover the pan and let cook for around 8 minutes, until the couscous has absorbed most of the water and is tender.

In a separate bowl, combine the honey, re-maining 1 Tbsp oil, vinegar, soy sauce, and salt and pepper to taste. When the vegetables are done, toss them with the couscous and drizzle the dressing over the top. Serve warm.

SAFFRON'S
FRESH BAO
8 BAO

I don't really feel it's my place to contribute to this collection, but it was awfully kind of Kaylee to ask me. These weren't nothing special to make. I learned the recipe in the maiden house, so I might be able to make a pleasing meal for my husband.

TIME
Prep: 10 minutes
Cook: 20 minutes

COURSE
Savory

DIETARY
Veg, Vegan

DIFFICULTY
Complex

INGREDIENTS	METHOD

1 batch bao dough, page 20
2 Tbsp sesame oil, for frying
½ small onion, diced
2 cloves garlic, minced
2 Tbsp red curry paste
2 tsp ground ginger
½ tsp cumin
Pinch spicy red pepper
10 oz button mushrooms
1 cup peas, canned or frozen
Salt and pepper, to taste

Make up the dough, then start on the filling so it's cool by the time the dough is done rising. Cook the onion and garlic in the oil in a frying pan over medium heat until they smell good and start to turn golden. Stir in the curry paste and the spices, then the mushrooms. Cook until the mushrooms let go of all their juice, then soak it back up again, around 5 minutes. Take off the heat and stir in the peas. Set the filling aside and let cool.

Once the dough has risen, divide it into 8 balls. Flatten each out into a disc about 3–4 inches across. Fill the middle with about ⅛ of the filling, then pinch the edges of the dough together in little overlapping pleats until the filling is entirely enclosed. Place each filled dumpling on a square of parchment paper and steam in a bamboo steamer for around 15–20 minutes. Let them sit off the heat, covered, for another 5 minutes before eating.

This woman is a dirty cheat, and I want this page out of the book. She tried to get us killed, you may remember.

yeah, but her bao were delicious...

螢火蟲

MAL'S
SHADOW SPARE RIBS
4+ SERVINGS

Back on the ranch on Shadow, before the Alliance bombed it into oblivion, Ma used to say of our cattle that we'd sell the best and eat the rest. I'll wager that was a bit of a stretch, seeing as there weren't no profit in eating the herd ourselves, but on occasion we would tuck into a particularly fine side of beef.

TIME
Marinate: 12+ hours
Cook: 1½ hours

COURSE
Savory

DIETARY
GF

DIFFICULTY
Easy

INGREDIENTS

¼ cup soy sauce
¼ cup rice wine
3 Tbsp brown sugar
1 tsp black pepper
¼ tsp ginger
1 clove garlic, minced
4 lb beef shortribs or pork spareribs

METHOD

Combine all the ingredients except the ribs in a plastic bag or bowl. Add the ribs and let marinate in the fridge for around 12 hours, or overnight.

When ready to cook, heat the oven to 350°F and set the ribs on a baking sheet lined with parchment paper. Bake 'em slow for 1½ hours, basting occasionally with the marinating juice. Serve hot.

螢火蟲

A nice yeasty beer pairs well with hot bao fresh from the steamer.

Bao are versatile and taste great with all kinds of fillings.

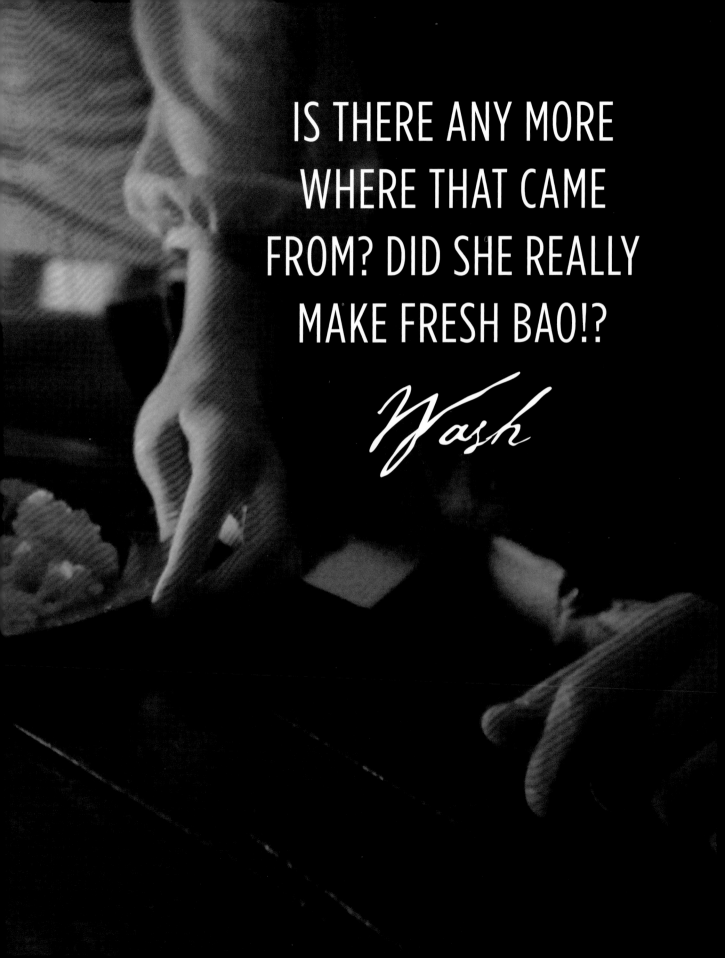

IS THERE ANY MORE WHERE THAT CAME FROM? DID SHE REALLY MAKE FRESH BAO!?

Wash

JAYNE'S
SPAGHETTI CASSEROLE
4 - 6 SERVINGS

See, if I gots to cook for everybody, then I'm gonna make it easy on myself. Me and Mattie could finish almost a whole batch between us, but Ma'd never let us. I miss my Ma's cooking somethin' fierce, but when I make this, it's like she's a little closer, you know?

TIME
Prep: 15 minutes
Cook: 30 minutes

COURSE
Savory

DIETARY
GF*

DIFFICULTY
Middling

INGREDIENTS

1 Tbsp olive oil
2–3 cloves garlic, minced
1 onion, diced
2 lb ground beef
1 tsp dried Italian seasoning
26 oz can crushed,
    fire-roasted tomatoes
8 oz uncooked spaghetti,
    broken in half
8 oz shredded mozzarella cheese
½ cup grated parmesan cheese

METHOD

In a large frying pan, heat the oil over medium heat. Add the garlic and onion and cook for a few minutes until brown. Add the beef and cook it 'til it's done. Drain the extra fat, then mix in the seasoning and the tomatoes.

Heat the oven to 350°F. Cook the spaghetti in a pot of water according to the directions on the packaging. Spread a thin layer of the sauce on the bottom of a casserole dish. Then yer gonna layer pasta, then mozzarella, then sauce, until it's all used up. Finish with sauce on top, then put the parmesan all over the top of that. Bake for 30 minutes, until the top is bubbly and a little brown.

螢火蟲

FRUITY OATY BARS

9 BARS

River has seemed... perturbed whenever she sees these bars for sale, even though she used to love them as a child. I've worked out this recipe to take their place, at least until we figure out what's wrong with the commercial ones. She'll eat these no problem, and a few other members of the crew have taken to them as well.

TIME
Prep: 5 minutes
Bake: 30 minutes

COURSE
Sweet

DIETARY
Veg, Vegan*

DIFFICULTY
Easy

INGREDIENTS

CRUST

1 cup flour
1 cup rolled oats
½ cup sugar
½ tsp ground cinnamon
¼ tsp baking powder
¼ tsp salt
8 Tbsp butter, melted

FILLING

1 cup diced dried apples
2 cups raspberry jam, warmed

METHOD

Preheat the oven to 350°F and lightly butter an 8 x 8 inch baking pan.

Combine all the ingredients for the crust in a food processor and pulse until you have a fine, crumb-like texture. Press about ⅔ of this mixture into the prepared pan, then bake for around 10 minutes.

Meanwhile, in a separate bowl, stir together the dried apples and warmed jam. When the bottom crust of the bars is done baking, spread the filling evenly over the pan. Top with the remaining crumb mixture and return to the oven for about 25 minutes, or until the top is lightly browned. Let the pan cool for at least 30 minutes before slicing into nine equal pieces.

螢火蟲

螢火蟲

Taste of Summer

makes
6–8
servings

Canned Peach Cobbler

Let Blue Sun Corporation bring the bounty of the border worlds right to your table!

Bursting with sweet, juicy flavor, these fresh peaches will make you feel the warmth of the sun on your face just as if you were enjoying a picnic in an orchard.

PREP: 10 MINUTES
BAKING: 5 MINUTES

DIETARY: VEG
CLASSIFICATION: SWEET
DIFFICULTY: EASY

INGREDIENTS:
2 CUPS BLUE SUN
    SLICED PEACHES
1 TSP FIVE-SPICE
1 CUP BLUE SUN
    SUGAR, DIVIDED
½ CUP BLUE SUN
    BUTTER, SOFTENED
1 LARGE EGG, OR
    BLUE SUN EGG
    SUBSTITUTE
1 TSP VANILLA
    EXTRACT
PINCH OF SALT
1 TSP BAKING POWDER
1 CUP BLUE SUN FLOUR

METHOD:
Preheat the oven to 350°F and lightly butter a pie pan.

Toss the peaches with the five-spice and 2 Tbsp sugar, then spread them out in the baking dish.

In a medium mixing bowl, beat together the remaining sugar and butter until pale and fluffy. Mix in the egg, vanilla, salt, and baking powder, then add the flour until just combined, which should make a pretty thick consistency. Using a large spoon, drop the topping in large dollops over the top of the peaches. Bake for around 35 minutes until the top is golden brown and the peaches are bubbling.

Tip! Enjoy alongside some Blue Sun vanilla ice cream!

SIMON'S

CHOCOLATE
PROTEIN CAKE

8 SERVINGS

Since I never had a chance to taste it, I asked Kaylee for the recipe she used to make my birthday cake. It's... interesting. Definitely not like something we would have eaten on Osiris, where we had easy access to flour and all the basic ingredients that usually go into a real cake. But I think I could come around to it, with time. Kaylee suggested I add some flour back into the recipe, though, to make it a little more... cake-like.

TIME
Prep: 10 minutes
Bake: 30 minutes

COURSE
Sweet

DIETARY
Veg

DIFFICULTY
Middling

INGREDIENTS

CAKE

4 Tbsp butter, melted
½ cup cocoa powder
15 oz can chickpeas,
    drained and rinsed
2 Tbsp hot water
3 eggs
½ cup sugar
4 Tbsp butter, melted
½ tsp salt
1 tsp baking soda
1 tsp vanilla extract
1 tsp ground cinnamon
1 cup flour
2 Tbsp vinegar

FROSTING

8 Tbsp butter, melted
½ cup unsweetened cocoa powder
3 cups powdered sugar
½ cup milk
1 tsp vanilla extract

METHOD

Preheat the oven to 350°F. Lightly butter a 9 inch round baking pan and dust with cocoa.

In a medium mixing bowl, puree the chickpeas with the hot water and eggs using an immersion blender. When the mixture is smooth, add in the sugar, butter, salt, baking soda, vanilla, cinnamon, and cocoa. Once this is all incorporated, add in the flour. Finally, quickly stir in the vinegar just before baking. Transfer the thick batter to the baking pan and move to the oven. Bake for about 25 minutes, until a toothpick inserted into the middle of the cake comes out clean.

When the cake is done, set the pan on a cooling rack until completely cooled. In the meantime, make up the frosting. Combine the melted butter and cocoa powder until you have a thick paste. Beat the mixture, alternately adding the powdered sugar and the milk until you have a consistency you like. Add the vanilla. Once the cake is completely cool, spread the frosting over it. Decorate with candles for a special occasion.

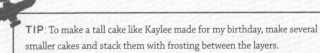

TIP: To make a tall cake like Kaylee made for my birthday, make several smaller cakes and stack them with frosting between the layers.

螢火蟲

Ceremonial tea set —————

Companions use tea
to help soothe and
relax their clients.

SIR,
THE COMPANION
GREETING CEREMONY
IS A RITUAL
WITH CENTURIES
OF TRADITION.

Inara

COMPANION TEA

During her train[...]many with varying degrees
of relaxing or aph[...] since he learned it. I don't
generally have to w[...]ts, but I still keep the more
expensive ones on[...]because it is so costly in the

TIME
Prep: 5 minutes

COURSE
Drink

DIETARY
GF, Veg, Vegan

DIFFICULTY
Easy

INGREDIENTS

1 tsp dried hibiscus flowers
1 cinnamon stick
Dash of vanilla extract
2 cups boiling water
Honey or sugar, to taste

METHOD

Place the hibiscus in a tea infuser and suspend in your mug of choice, along with the cinnamon stick. Pour the boiling water over both and allow to steep for up to 5 minutes. Remove the infuser and cinnamon stick, add a dash of vanilla, then sweeten to taste.

MAL'S

HAYMAKER'S PUNCH

ENOUGH FOR MANY SERVINGS

This here drinking vinegar is pretty common out in the Border worlds, especially wherever you find folk doing hard labor of the agricultural sort. Makes sense, as folk can pretty much make all the elements of it themselves, with no need for ingredients bought from the Alliance. It's a mighty refreshing drink that goes down easy on a hot working day.

TIME
Prep: 5 minutes
Steep: Overnight

COURSE
Drink

DIETARY
GF, Veg, Vegan

DIFFICULTY
Easy

INGREDIENTS

1 cup apple cider vinegar
1 cup maple syrup
1–2 inches fresh ginger, sliced thin,
*   or ½ tsp powdered ginger*
Water, to cut it, to taste

METHOD

Combine the vinegar and maple syrup in a glass bottle, then add the ginger. Let the mixture steep overnight, then dilute to taste with water. I like a ratio of at least 3 Tbsp concentrate for every 8 oz of water and, if the work's done for the day, add some ice while you put your feet up.

Variations: I've heard tell of some folks using sugar, molasses, or honey if they can't come by maple syrup. All manner of herbs and spice is also fair game, and makes for a more healthful brew.

This makes sense — the vinegar would provide electrolytes, while the sweetener would give an immediate boost to energy.

RECIPES FROM THE BORDER & BEYOND

MAL'S
CORN DODGERS
18 DODGERS

If you need a quick bite that's easy to make over a fire, then this here's for you. It's been popular among settlers on the Border worlds as well as with them with a mind to soldiering. I've seen all sorts of variants, depending on what folks have available, like cheese, peppers, chili, whole corn, bacon, and the like. These are the essentials, fit for making between traveling or fighting. In peacetime, I like 'em dipped in some honey or sweet chili sauce.

TIME
Prep: 5 minutes
Rest: 20 minutes
Fry: 15 minutes

COURSE
Snack

DIETARY
GF, Veg*, Vegan*

DIFFICULTY
Easy

INGREDIENTS

2 cups ground cornmeal
½ tsp salt, plus extra
1 Tbsp bacon grease, plus extra
1½ cups boiling water

METHOD

Combine the cornmeal and salt in a medium mixing bowl and stir in the bacon grease. Pour the boiling water over and stir it all up. Let it sit for 20 minutes or so.

Scoop a couple of tablespoons worth of the batter into your hand and form into a flattened oval, sorta the shape of an ear of corn, about 2–3 inches long and 1 inch wide. Repeat with the rest of the batter. Heat a frying pan over medium-low heat on the fire or your stove and add a little bacon grease. When it's hot, fill the pan with dodgers, not crowding them too close. Fry for around 8 minutes on the first side, then flip for another 5 or so. The dodgers should be a nice crisped brown on each side. They're great on their own, but better with a dipping sauce. If you've got it, sprinkle with a little extra salt before eating.

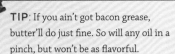

TIP: If you ain't got bacon grease, butter'll do just fine. So will any oil in a pinch, but won't be as flavorful.

ZOE'S

STEAMED PUMPKIN BUNS

8 BAO

I was born on a ship, so you might say I've got flying in my blood, so to speak. It at least accounts for my attraction to pilots, terrible moustaches notwithstanding. But all that time on a ship gives a person an appreciation for simple, good food. You can get some of that shipboard, if you're clever with ingredients, but nothing beats good country cooking. These sweet little buns are pretty common out at the Border, and I like to buy a couple whenever they turn up.

TIME
Prep: 15 minutes
Steam: 40 minutes

COURSE
Snack

DIETARY
Veg, Vegan

DIFFICULTY
Complex

INGREDIENTS

1 batch bao dough,
        adapted, page 20

FILLING

9 oz pumpkin puree
¼ cup brown sugar
1 tsp cornstarch
1 tsp five-spice

METHOD

While the bao dough is rising, make the filling. Combine the pumpkin puree, sugar, cornstarch, and five-spice in a medium pan over medium heat. Stir occasionally and cook for 5–10 minutes, until noticeably thickened. Remove from heat and allow to cool.

When the dough has risen, divide it into 8 equal pieces. Roll each piece of dough into a ball, then flatten to a disc about 4–5 inches across. Place a 2 Tbsp dollop of filling into the middle of the disc, then pinch the edges shut and place seam side down on a cupcake liner or square of parchment. Steam in a bamboo steamer for about 20 minutes and enjoy warm.

萤火虫

ZOE'S
GARLIC GRIDDLE BREAD

8 SERVINGS

Times are you don't have an oven to bake in, or a stove to cook on, so you've got to go back to how humans have always cooked: over the fire. We might sail through the stars now, but it all started with fire and bread. All you need for that is some heat and dough, and you'll be fed in no time.

TIME
Prep: 10 minutes
Fry: 15 minutes

COURSE
Snack

DIETARY
Veg*

DIFFICULTY
Middling

INGREDIENTS

Oil for frying
2 cups flour
2 tsp baking soda
1 tsp salt
1–2 cloves garlic, minced
½ cup parmesan cheese, halved
¾ cups milk

METHOD

Combine the dry ingredients in a medium mixing bowl along with the minced garlic and half the cheese. Gradually stir in the milk until you have a nice dough that isn't too wet. Turn out on a lightly floured surface and knead for several minutes, until soft and pliable. Divide the dough into 8 equal pieces and press flat between your hands.

Pour a little oil in a frying pan or griddle pan over medium heat. When the oil is shimmering, lay a couple pieces of dough on the pan at a time. Fry for about a minute, until golden brown, then flip and repeat on the other side. Move to a nearby plate when done and sprinkle with a little extra cheese.

ZOE'S

GARLIC GREEN BEANS
4 SERVINGS

Fresh greens can be hard to come by, and the canned stuff can be a mite unpalatable at times, but even canned green beans ain't never tasted so good as when you cook 'em real hot with spice and plenty of garlic.

TIME
Prep: 10 minutes

COURSE
Savory

DIETARY
GF, Veg, Vegan

DIFFICULTY
Easy

INGREDIENTS	METHOD

2 Tbsp sesame oil
1 pound green beans,
    stems cut off
2–3 cloves garlic, minced
2 Tbsp soy sauce
1 Tbsp rice vinegar
1 tsp brown sugar
¼ cup water
½ tsp crushed red
    pepper flakes

Pour the sesame oil into a large frying pan and bring to medium-high heat. Add the green beans and cook for 5 minutes, until they are browning and starting to look a little worse for wear. Add the garlic and cook for another minute or so, until it's browned and fragrant. Add the remaining ingredients and cook for a final minute or two, until the liquids have mostly been absorbed. Serve straight away.

TIP: For some extra zing, serve with the sweet chili sauce from page 19.

螢火蟲

BACON & CHEESE TOAST

2 SERVINGS

Golly, this has *got* to be one of my very favorite snacks. Whenever I have one of those tricky mechanical problems that's a real doozy, I like to make a couple helpings of this to keep me going

TIME
Prep: 5 minutes
Cook: 10 minutes

COURSE
Savory

DIETARY
GF*

DIFFICULTY
Easy

INGREDIENTS

2–3 Tbsp milk
1 egg
½ tsp baking powder
4 oz grated cheese
Salt and pepper to taste
4 slices bacon, cooked to crispy
2 slices bread of choice, toasted

METHOD

In a small bowl, beat together the milk, egg, baking powder, cheese, and salt and pepper. Lay the bacon over the slices of toast and top with the egg mixture. Slide under the broiler and cook until puffy and brown, around 5 minutes.

TIP: For extra crispy bacon, cook it on a cooling rack set on a rimmed baking sheet at 400°F for around 20 minutes.

螢火蟲

JAYNE'S
PORK HASH
4 - 6 SERVINGS

This is my best breakfast recipe. You can cook it however you like. I always liked mine real crispy, but Ma cooked hers less, and stirred some cheese in right after it was done. I like the cheese part, but it's gotta be crispy. Used to have this growing up, and look at me now: big and strong.

TIME
Prep: 5 minutes
Cook: 10 minutes

COURSE
Savory

DIETARY
GF

DIFFICULTY
Middling

INGREDIENTS

1 cup white or yellow cornmeal
1 cup whole milk
1 Tbsp brown sugar
1 tsp salt
1 ½ cups boiling water
1 lb pork sausage, cooked,
        drained and crumbled
lots of butter

METHOD

Lightly grease a loaf pan and put it nearby.

Mix up the cornmeal, milk, sugar, and salt real good in a saucepan. Put it on medium heat, and pour in the boiling water. Cook it until it's real thick and all bubbly-like. Oh, and you gotta stir it some. I dunno, like, 5 minutes? Then take it off the heat and mix in the sausage. Shift it all over into the loaf pan and chill until you're ready to eat.

To really cook it, melt butter in a frying pan over medium-high heat. Scoop out as much of the hash as you're gonna eat, then cook it in the butter. Stir it around some, until it's how you like it (crispy!). Eat it with eggs, if you got 'em.

螢火蟲

WASH'S
CHICKEN & DUMPLINGS
6 - 8 SERVINGS

All those bits of meat and veg floating around biscuit islands in a sea of creamy sauce. It makes me feel like a god looming over a tiny realm, scooping up unsuspecting carrots and devouring them.

TIME
Prep: 20 minutes
Cook: 35 minutes

COURSE
Savory

DIETARY
N/A

DIFFICULTY
Complex

INGREDIENTS

4 cups chicken broth
½ tsp dried savory, or other herbs,
    to taste
2 large chicken breasts, boneless
    and skinless,
    cut into 2 inch pieces
1 cup mixed vegetables
Pinch black pepper
1 batch white sauce, page 18
1 batch biscuits, page 23

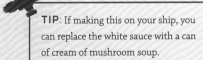

TIP: If making this on your ship, you can replace the white sauce with a can of cream of mushroom soup.

METHOD

Preheat the oven to 350°F and set out a large casserole dish. Pour the chicken broth into a medium saucepan over medium-high heat and bring to a boil. Add in the herbs and chicken breast, then let simmer for about 10 minutes. Add in the vegetables and a pinch of black pepper, and simmer for a further 10 minutes.

While the chicken and veg are cooking, make your white sauce and biscuits. Once the chicken's done, remove it from the heat. If you'd like a finer consistency, you can shred the chicken into bite-size pieces, but that isn't necessary. Strain out the chicken and vegetables and transfer to the casserole dish, making sure to reserve the chicken broth left behind. Pour the white sauce over the chicken, then top up with the reserved chicken stock. Add the biscuit dough to the top of everything in large dollops, then bake for around 35 minutes. Allow to cool for 10 minutes before serving.

螢火蟲

MAL'S
PORK & BEANS
6 - 8 SERVINGS

Ain't nothing more fitting for a traveling type of meal than pork and beans. The beans are canned, the bacon's cured, and everything gets cooked up low and slow over a fire 'til it's nice and thick. Time was, this was the main sort of meal you might see in a week, moving cattle out on a ranch. Can't say as I miss that life, but time and again I get a real hankering for a big mess of this.

TIME
Prep: 15 minutes
Bake: 2 hours

COURSE
Savory

DIETARY
GF

DIFFICULTY
Easy

INGREDIENTS

1 lb bacon
1 onion, diced
30 oz canned kidney beans
4 Tbsp ketchup
¼ cup molasses
⅔ cup brown sugar
¼ cup cider vinegar
1 tsp five-spice

METHOD

Preheat the oven to 400°F and set the bacon on a cooling rack over a rimmed baking sheet. Cook until just shy of crispy, about 15 minutes or so. Let cool and crumble or cut into small pieces.

Pour about 2 Tbsp of the bacon grease into a frying pan and cook the onion for about 5 minutes, 'til it's soft and golden. Add in the beans, ketchup, molasses, brown sugar, vinegar, and spice, then let it simmer for a minute or so. Move everything to a casserole dish, along with the bacon. Mix it up real well and bake it for about 2 hours, or a little more if you want it thicker.

Tasty with some sautéed greens and whatever meat you've had roasting over the fire.

螢火蟲

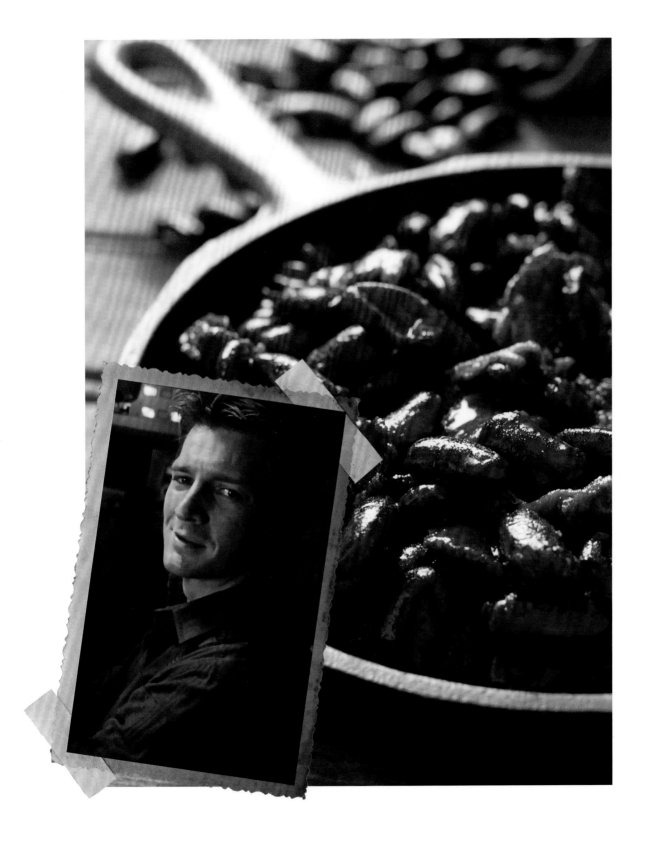

螢火蟲 FROM BEYOND THE BORDER 79

WASH'S
GOAT CURRY
4 SERVINGS

He had a bad experience. Once.

Have you ever met a goat? They're these beady-eyed little creatures who'll soon as bite you as look at you. And let me tell you, they'll eat anything. The only way to be safe is to eat them first. It's a man-eat-goat world.

TIME
Prep: 15 minutes
Cook: 2 hours

COURSE
Savory

DIETARY
GF

DIFFICULTY
Easy

INGREDIENTS

3 Tbsp vegetable oil
1 lb goat meat, cubed
2 cloves garlic, minced
1 medium onion, diced
2 Tbsp curry powder
1 tsp thyme
1 Tbsp tomato paste
1 large potato, cubed
Spicy pepper, to taste
Salt, to taste

METHOD

Heat the oil in a medium saucepan over medium heat, then add the meat and brown it all over. Then add the garlic and onion and cook for another minute or so. Add in the curry powder, thyme, and tomato paste, then add around 3 cups of water, or enough to cover the meat completely. Cook for 1½ hours, until the meat is very tender. Add the cubed potato and cook for another 20 minutes or so. Give it a taste, and tweak the seasoning accordingly. It's extra good served over some savory rice.

螢火蟲

MAL'S
MAMA REYNOLDS' SHOOFLY PIE

8 SERVINGS

Mama wouldn't brook no nonsense or fussing over her big dinner table, so when all the season's fresh fruit was gone, and the preserved fruit as well, this pie used to keep the peace among all the farmhands. I conjure it's even finer than any apple confection, no matter how sweet the fruit might be.

TIME
Prep: 10 minutes
Bake: 35 minutes

COURSE
Sweet

DIETARY
Veg

DIFFICULTY
Middling

INGREDIENTS

1 batch pastry dough, page 20
1 cup flour
⅔ cup brown sugar
Pinch of salt
6 Tbsp butter, chilled
1 egg
1 cup molasses
½ cup cold water
¼ cup hot water
1 tsp baking soda

METHOD

Preheat the oven to 350°F. Roll out your chilled pie dough to about ¼ inch thick and gently drape over a pie pan, trimming off any excess and crimping the edges.

In a large mixing bowl, combine the flour, brown sugar, and salt. Rub in the butter until you have a consistency like breadcrumbs. Divide this crumble mixture and set half aside as the topping for the pie.

In a separate small bowl, mix together the egg, molasses, and cold water. Combine the hot water and baking soda, then add this to the molasses mixture along with half the crumble. Pour the molasses mix into the pie pan, then gently top with the other half of the flour crumble. Bake for 35 minutes, at which point the pie should be set on the edges, but still wobbly in the middle. Remove from the oven and let cool completely before slicing.

螢火蟲

COULDN'T GET AHOLD OF NO FLOUR, SO IT'S MOSTLY PROTEIN. IN FACT, IT'S PRETTY MUCH WHAT WE JUST HAD FOR DINNER...

Kaylee

BREAD PUDDING

16 ROLLS

Isn't it amazing how, with a little ingenuity and good ingredients, you can take something that's no longer good and make it into something delicious? When you grow up on a planet so squished full with people that you can't see the sky, you learn to make do with what you've got. Our version of bread pudding wasn't as glamorous as this, but trust me that this version is much tastier.

TIME
Prep: 10 minutes
Bake: 35 minutes

COURSE
Sweet

DIETARY
Veg

DIFFICULTY
Middling

INGREDIENTS

8 cups stale challah bread, cubed
½ cup raisins
3 eggs
1 cup heavy cream
2 cups milk
¼ cup brown sugar
¼ cup white sugar
1 tsp vanilla
1 tsp cardamom
2 Tbsp butter, melted

METHOD

Preheat oven to 350°F and lightly butter an 8 x 8 inch square baking dish. Spread the cubed bread and raisins out evenly in the dish, pressing down to compact.

In a separate bowl, beat together the eggs, cream, milk, sugar, vanilla, and cardamom. Pour this over the bread in the dish and allow to soak it up for around 5–10 minutes. Press gently down again, then pour the butter over the top and bake for 35 minutes, or until cooked through and browning on top.

The bread works best if it's a day or so old. The recipe is also fantastic served alongside some ice cream, and the caramel sauce on page 116–117.

SIMON'S
MOLASSES TAFFY TWISTS
24 CANDIES

So, River took a liking to this candy when we were held captive by those lunatic townspeople in Jiangyin. They didn't have much, so I suppose this was a special treat for them. They could have done worse — at least molasses has some nutritional value.

WITCH CANDY!

TIME
Cook: 15 minutes
Pull: 20 minutes

COURSE
Dessert

DIETARY
GF, Veg, Vegan*

DIFFICULTY
Complex

INGREDIENTS

1 cup sugar
½ cup molasses (not blackstrap)
3 Tbsp water
1 tsp white vinegar
1 Tbsp butter, plus more
        for hands and tools
¼ tsp baking soda

METHOD

Lay out a silicone mat on your work surface, or butter a large baking sheet. Stir together the sugar, molasses, water, and vinegar in a small saucepan over medium-high heat. Let the mixture cook for 15 minutes or so until it reaches 260°F, hard-ball stage. Remove from the heat and quickly stir in the butter and baking soda. Pour this mixture onto your prepared work surface, then go rinse the pot and your tools in hot water before the sugar hardens.

Butter a spatula and use it to move the molasses mixture around to start cooling it, taking care as hot sugar can burn easily. Once the taffy is starting to lift from the surface and is cool enough to touch, it's ready to pull. Thoroughly butter both hands, then take hold of the taffy. Stretch it out about two feet, then double it over and continue to stretch and twist as you go. After several minutes, it should be light golden in color and increasingly less sticky to the touch. Double and twist, drawing the taffy out into a rope about ½ inch wide. Lightly butter a sharp knife or pair of kitchen shears and snip into pieces 1–2 inches long. Wrap each piece in waxed paper or candy wrappers, and store in an airtight container.

STRAWBERRY SHORTCAKE

12 SERVINGS

Them rich Core world folks might be able to grow fruits whenever they want but, out in the Border, growin's still real seasonal: if you miss the strawberry season, it's over until the next one. When I was growin' up, the strawberry festival was something we looked forward to all year. Only lasted a little while but, for those coupla weeks, the whole center of town smelled like strawberries. Everybody'd make 'em into jam, pies, whatever you could think of, but my favorite was the shortcake.

TIME
Prep: 5 minutes
Bake: 15 minutes

COURSE
Sweet

DIETARY
Veg

DIFFICULTY
Easy

INGREDIENTS

1 batch biscuit dough,
page 23
6 cups sliced strawberries
¼ cup sugar, plus extra
1 cup heavy cream

METHOD

Preheat the oven to 425°F and set out a baking sheet. Make the biscuits, following the modified recipe on page 23. When the biscuits are in the oven, put the strawberries in a big bowl and shake the sugar all over 'em. Let that sit until the biscuits are done. Whip up the cream and a little sugar to stiff peaks and put somewhere cool.

To serve, slice the biscuits in half, and give each one a good dollop of whipped cream and a whole heap of strawberries over the top. Tastes like summertime!

INARA'S

BORDER BERRY CORDIAL

1 BATCH

Near as I could tell, this was the only appealing drink to look at in the whole bar on Santo, and that's being generous. It had a pleasant, creamy tartness, even if it was a little rough. It seems the barkeep is a man of some talent, wasted, perhaps, on a backwater such as that. Amazing how some people manage to live their dreams, no matter what hardships life throws at them.

TIME
Prep: 10 minutes
Steep: 3 hours

COURSE
Drink

DIETARY
GF, Veg, Vegan

DIFFICULTY
Easy

INGREDIENTS

1 cup sugar
1 cup water
¼ cup raspberries
2–3 Tbsp hibiscus flowers
1 14 oz can coconut milk
1 cup vodka, higher the proof the better

METHOD

Combine the sugar, water, raspberries, and hibiscus in a small saucepan over medium heat and cook for 5–10 minutes, until the sugar has dissolved and the berries are soft. Mash the berries, then add the coconut milk and stir until it is completely incorporated. Finally, stir in the vodka and let the whole mixture steep for about 3 hours in the fridge to let the flavors strengthen. Strain into a clean bottle or jar and store in the fridge for up to a month.

螢火蟲

MULLED WINE

4 SERVINGS

Warming to the core, variations of this drink can be found throughout the 'Verse, but this one struck me as particularly pleasant. The sweetness helps to smooth rough country red wine, and it is often served at festive occasions. A word to the wise: although I'm one for marriages between two fully consenting adults, recipes such as this have been used on some Border worlds to marry away kinfolk to unsuspecting off-worlders or residents of the next village over.

TIME
Prep: 5 minutes
Cook: 30 minutes

COURSE
Drink

DIETARY
GF, Veg, Vegan

DIFFICULTY
Easy

INGREDIENTS

½ cup sugar or honey

25 fl oz bottle red wine

6 cinnamon sticks

2 whole star anise

6 whole cloves

1 tsp fennel seeds

1 cup brandy

½ apple, cored and diced

10 oz can mandarin orange
    slices in juice

METHOD

Combine the sugar and red wine in a medium saucepan over medium-low heat. Stir for several minutes, until the sugar has dissolved, then turn the heat down a little more, so it never quite reaches a simmer.

Add the cinnamon sticks straight to the pot. Combine the anise, cloves, and fennel seeds in a small cloth bag or tea strainer, and suspend in the wine. Let it infuse for about 30 minutes. In the last 10 minutes of steeping, add the brandy, diced apple, and both the orange slices and their juice. Bring back up to just under a simmer, then remove from heat. Discard the spices and serve wine topped with fruit in heat-proof mugs.

ALL THE PROTEIN, VITAMINS, AND CARBS OF YOUR GRANDMA'S BEST TURKEY DINNER, PLUS FIFTEEN PERCENT ALCOHOL.

Jayne

The ancient Egyptians, back on Earth-That-Was, used a similar form of beer to mudder's milk called liquid bread. They fed it to the slaves who built their pyramids. It kept the slaves from starving, and knocked them out at night, so they wouldn't be inclined to insurrection.

Real mudder's milk can
contain up to 2% mud.

JAYNE'S
MUDDER'S MILK
BUNCH OF SERVINGS

Might be I've got all sorts of mixed-up feelings about Canton, and how they's thinkin' I'm some kinda hero. I ain't no gorram hero, got it? Their mudder's milk goes down real easy, though, no mind what some sissy like Wash says. Just don't go doin' 'em any kinda favors, or they'll never let you forget it.

TIME
Cook: 15 minutes

COURSE
Drink

DIETARY
GF, Veg

DIFFICULTY
Complex

INGREDIENTS

½ cup rolled oats,
    soaked overnight
    in 1 cup water
1 cup cream
¼ cup malt syrup
¼ cup brown sugar
3 egg yolks
½–1 cup rum
2 cups stout beer

METHOD

Combine the soaked oats, cream, and malt syrup in a medium saucepan and blend with an immersion blender. Add the sugar and bring up to a simmer, stirring occasionally until the sugar is dissolved.

Beat the egg yolks in a small bowl, then, while beating, pour in a thin stream of the hot cream mixture, just enough to temper the eggs so they don't scramble when you tip 'em into the main drink. Pour the egg mix into the saucepan, whisking the whole time. Cook for 5–10 minutes, until noticeably thickened. Add the rum and beer, and mix for another minute or so. Drink it warm or cold.

RECIPES FROM THE CORE WORLDS, UPPER CRUST

SWEET POTATO BITES
MAKES 2 DOZEN BITES

PREP: 10 MINUTES
COOKING: 20 MINUTES

DIETARY: GF, VEG, VEGAN
CLASSIFICATION: SNACK

INGREDIENTS:
2 SLENDER BLUE SUN
    SWEET POTATOES,
    CLEANED AND SLICED INTO
    ¼ INCH THICK PIECES
2 TBSP BLUE SUN OLIVE OIL
½ TSP CUMIN
½ TSP PAPRIKA,
    PLUS MORE FOR DUSTING
SALT, TO TASTE
1 BLUE SUN AVOCADO
1 TBSP RICE WINE VINEGAR
½ TSP SALT
SEVERAL BLUE SUN CHERRY
    TOMATOES, SLICED THIN

Preheat your oven to 400ºF and set out a baking sheet.

Combine the sweet potato slices, olive oil, spices, and salt in a medium mixing bowl and toss to make sure the potatoes are evenly coated. Bake for about 20 minutes, or until tender. Move sweet potato slices to a serving platter.

In a separate bowl, mash the avocado to a fine consistency, then stir in the vinegar and salt. Place a dollop of the avocado mixture on each potato slice, then top with a small slice of cherry tomato. Sprinkle with a little extra paprika and serve straight away.

STUFFED MUSHROOMS

MAKES A DOZEN

Preheat the oven to 350ºF and set out a baking sheet.

Separate the stems from the mushrooms, and place the tops on a baking sheet, hollow side up. Dice the stems along with the shallot. Melt 1 Tbsp butter in a frying pan, then add the chopped mushroom stems, shallot, and garlic. Cook for several minutes, until soft and fragrant. Stir in the sesame oil, curry paste, and rice wine for another minute or so, then remove from heat and add the breadcrumbs. Divide this mixture among the mushroom caps, pressing it into the openings and heaping it up where possible. Bake for 15 minutes, and serve warm.

PREP: 10 MINUTES
COOKING: 15 MINUTES

DIETARY: VEGAN *
CLASSIFICATION: SNACK
DIFFICULTY: MIDDLING

INGREDIENTS:
8 OZ BUTTON MUSHROOMS
1 SHALLOT
1 CLOVE GARLIC, MINCED
1 TBSP BUTTER
1 TSP SESAME OIL
½ TSP RED CURRY PASTE
1 TBSP RICE WINE
2 TBSP PANKO BREADCRUMBS

TOFU CUBES

ENOUGH FOR A SMALL PARTY

PREP: 5 MINUTES
COOKING: 20 MINUTES

DIETARY: GF, VEG
CLASSIFICATION: SNACK
DIFFICULTY: EASY

INGREDIENTS:
2 TBSP HONEY
2 TBSP SOY SAUCE
2 TBSP LIME JUICE
2 TBSP SESAME OIL
1 POUND TOFU, EXTRA
   FIRM, DRAINED AND
   CUT INTO 1INCH CUBES
1 TBSP SESAME SEEDS
SEVERAL CHERRY
   TOMATOES, SLICED THIN

Whisk together the honey, soy sauce, lime juice, and sesame oil in a small bowl. Marinate the tofu cubes for at least two hours, then arrange on a baking sheet and broil for a minute or so, until slightly crisped on the outside. Sprinkle with sesame seeds, then top each with a slice of cherry tomato. Add a drop or two more soy sauce on that, and serve.

蟹醬
Crab Dip

NOTHING SAYS "GOOD PARTY" LIKE A DELICIOUS DISH TO SHARE! WHETHER YOU ARE HOST OR GUEST, THIS DISH MAKES A THOUGHTFUL ADDITION TO ANY BANQUET SPREAD.

MAKES ENOUGH FOR A SMALL PARTY

PREP: 5 MINUTES
COOKING: 20 MINUTES

DIETARY: GF
CLASSIFICATION: SNACK
DIFFICULTY: EASY

INGREDIENTS:
8 oz cream cheese, softened
¼ cup heavy cream
½ tsp soy sauce
Splash rice wine vinegar
2 cloves garlic, minced
2 tsp sugar
Pinch of salt
1¼ cup of mild cheddar cheese
16 oz lump or imitation crab meat
¼ red bell pepper, diced
1 small bunch scallions, diced

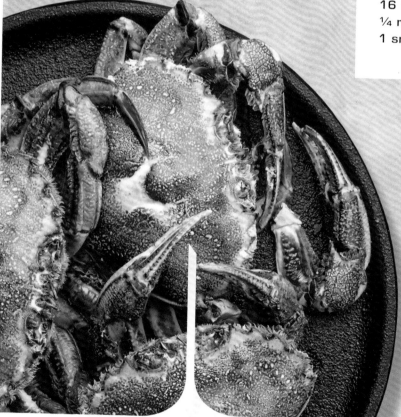

Preheat the oven to 400ºF and set out a medium oven-safe dish.

Beat together the cream cheese, heavy cream, soy sauce, vinegar, garlic, sugar, and salt in a medium mixing bowl. Mix in the remaining ingredients, then transfer over to the baking dish. Bake for around 20 minutes, until bubbling and hot. Serve with crackers or bread cubes.

INARA'S
LOTUS CHIPS
1 - 2 SERVINGS

Do you know the feeling when you just want to snack on something, even though you're not hungry? These chips are for moments like those, because they satisfy those cravings with their salty crunch. But there's not much to them, so you don't need to feel guilty about your snack on the side.

TIME
Prep: 5 minutes
Bake: 20 minutes

COURSE
Snack

DIETARY
GF, Veg, Vegan

DIFFICULTY
Easy

INGREDIENTS

*2 large lotus roots, peeled
    and sliced very thin*
2 Tbsp olive oil
1 tsp toasted sesame oil
Salt and pepper to taste

METHOD

Preheat oven to 325°F and set out a baking sheet.

In a medium bowl, toss the lotus slices with olive oil, sesame oil, salt, and pepper. Spread the lotus slices evenly on the baking sheet in a single layer, then bake for around 20 minutes or until they are turning brown and crunchy. Transfer to a plate lined with paper towel to drain any excess oil.

INARA'S
MANDARIN SALAD
4 SERVINGS

I know there are certain stereotypes about a lady only ordering a salad on a date, but every so often I just crave fresh greens. And one of the luxuries of dining in the Core is an abundance of fresh fruits and vegetables. This salad is one I often order, given the chance. It feels clean and healthy.

TIME
Prep: 10 minutes

COURSE
Savory

DIETARY
GF, Veg, Vegan*

DIFFICULTY
Easy

INGREDIENTS

1 apple, cored
10 oz can mandarin oranges,
        juice reserved
10 oz mixed greens
½ cup cooked shelled edamame
½ cup crumbled goat cheese
¼ cup candied walnuts

DRESSING

½ cup olive oil
Half reserved juice from mandarins
2 Tbsp honey
1 Tbsp rice wine vinegar
2 tsp poppy seeds

METHOD

Thinly slice the apples and toss with half the juice from the mandarins. Set the remaining juice aside for the dressing.

In a large serving bowl, toss the greens, mandarin slices, apple slices, edamame, cheese, and candied nuts. In a separate bottle or jar, combine the ingredients for the dressing and shake vigorously. Drizzle the dressing over the salad just before serving.

螢火蟲

螢火蟲

SIMON'S
ROAST DUCK
4 SERVINGS

There was a place near where River and I grew up that had the most amazing duck. Our father used to pick one up sometimes on his way home from work. I loved the crispy, colorful skin and the richness of the meat.

TIME
Prep: 10 minutes
Cook: 1½–2 hours

COURSE
Savory

DIETARY
GF

DIFFICULTY
Complex

INGREDIENTS

1 duck, about 4–5 lb
1 Tbsp oil
Salt, to taste
1 lemon, sliced thin
2 cinnamon sticks
½ cup pomegranate
        juice
¼ cup plum wine
¼ cup orange juice
1 Tbsp sugar
1 Tbsp ground ginger
2 star anise
Pinch ground cinnamon
Pomegranate seeds
        (optional)

METHOD

Preheat the oven to 400°F and set out a roasting pan.

Pat the duck dry and prick it all over the breast area to help the fat run off. Rub lightly with oil to help the skin brown, sprinkle with a little salt, then fill with the sliced lemon and cinnamon sticks.

In a small saucepan, combine the remaining ingredients, except the pomegranate seeds, and bring up to just a simmer, then remove from heat. Pour this over the duck, then move the roasting pan to the oven. Cook for around 1½ hours, or longer depending on the size of your bird, basting occasionally, and covering with foil if it starts to get too brown. When done, move to a serving platter and let rest for a few minutes before scattering over the pomegranate seeds and carving. Excellent with plum sauce on the side.

螢火蟲

螢火蟲

INARA'S

SPICED LAMB
2 - 4 SERVINGS

One thing I miss most about House Madrassa is the food. Every day we had a luxurious spread, with all manner of different fruits, meats, and desserts. Of course, much of it was to train us how to properly eat those things, but I never tired of the variety.

TIME
Prep: 10 minutes
Cook: 10+ minutes

COURSE
Savory

DIETARY
GF

DIFFICULTY
Middling

INGREDIENTS

1 Tbps sugar
¼ cup pistachios, shelled
1 tsp ground cinnamon
½ tsp cumin
1 lb lamb, cubed
2 Tbsp pomegranate molasses

METHOD

Preheat the oven to 400°F. Combine the sugar, pistachios, and spices in a food processor and pulse until you have a fine consistency. Transfer to a shallow bowl and set aside.

Thread the lamb onto skewers — on Sihnon, they use a sort of ornamental sword, as metal is best — and baste with the pomegranate molasses. Place on a baking sheet and cook in the oven for for 8–10 minutes, or until cooked to your liking. Turn the kebabs once during cooking to ensure that they are browned on all sides. Excellent served alongside rice or couscous.

螢火蟲

RIVER'S
SAFFRON RICE PUDDING
2 - 4 SERVINGS

It's golden, but not gold. Not Au, not 79. The gold is from the stamen of saffron flowers, *crocus sativus*, in the *Iridaceae* family. And rice: edible seeds of the grass species *oryza sativa*. *Sativus* and *sativa*, an harmonious combination.

TIME
Prep: 20 minutes

COURSE
Sweet

DIETARY
GF, Veg, Vegan*

DIFFICULTY
Easy

INGREDIENTS

4 cups milk
½ cup rice
¼ cup honey
Pinch saffron
½ tsp five-spice mix
Dash of vanilla extract

METHOD

Combine milk, rice, honey, saffron, and five-spice in a medium saucepan. Simmer on medium-low for about 15–20 minutes, until rice is soft. Remove from heat and stir in the vanilla. Serve warm.

Note: They make a simpler version of this on a number of the Border planets without saffron or vanilla, using whatever spice they've got. I've seen big pots of it during a village celebration, since it's real simple to make in big quantities.

螢火蟲

MATCHA MACARON DROPS

24 MERINGUES

These were among my favorite treats growing up. In fact, I almost always had some on hand when studying for exams, even after I went to medical school. I suppose I'm a little nostalgic for those times, even given the terrible events that came after.

TIME
Prep: 15 minutes
Bake: 1½ hours

COURSE
Sweet

DIETARY
GF, Veg

DIFFICULTY
Middling

INGREDIENTS

3 egg whites, room temperature
⅔ cup granulated sugar
½ tsp cream of tartar
Pinch salt
1 Tbsp matcha powder
Green food coloring (optional)

METHOD

Preheat your oven to 200°F and line a baking sheet with either parchment paper or a silicone mat. Begin simmering about 1 inch of water in a small saucepan on the stove.

In a separate medium mixing bowl, combine the egg whites and sugar. Place this bowl on top of the pan with simmering water and begin beating the eggs with an electric mixer. After a couple of minutes, the mixture should be warm, and the sugar should have dissolved. Remove from heat, add the cream of tartar and salt, and continue to beat for 5–10 minutes more, until it forms stiff peaks. Beat in the matcha powder and food coloring (if you're using it), then transfer to a piping bag fitted with a large star tip. Pipe dollops of the meringue onto the prepared baking sheet. Bake for 1½ hours, then turn off the oven and leave the pan in, with the door closed, for another hour or so to cool.

螢火蟲

...CED
...AKE

I was first intro... ...to a little bakery he owned on Osiris. The flavors re... ...House, and I was surprised by the feeling of nost... ...of his recipe, insisted on showing me how they wer... ...myself later. As long as I don't name names, I don't suppose this violates the companion code of confidentiality...

TIME
Prep: 10 minutes
Steam: 30 minutes

COURSE
Sweet

DIETARY
Veg

DIFFICULTY
Middling

INGREDIENTS

2 Tbsp vegetable oil, plus extra
3 eggs
⅓ cup brown sugar
1 Tbsp rose water
½ tsp vanilla extract
1 heaping tsp ground ginger
½ tsp cardamom
1 tsp baking soda
½ tsp baking powder
1 cup flour

METHOD

Line an 8 inch bamboo steamer with a disc of parchment paper, and set a pot to simmer with 2–3 inches of water in it; the pot should be small enough that the steamer can sit on top of it without touching the water. Lightly brush the inside of the steamer lid with vegetable oil to keep the cake from sticking.

In a medium mixing bowl, beat together the eggs and brown sugar for around 2 minutes, until pale and fluffy. Add the rose water, oil, vanilla, ginger, cardamom, baking soda, and baking powder, then beat for another minute. Gently fold in the flour, then pour the batter into the prepared steamer. Put the lid on the steamer and set it over the now simmering water. Steam for around 30 minutes, or until a toothpick inserted into the middle of the cake comes out clean.

螢火蟲

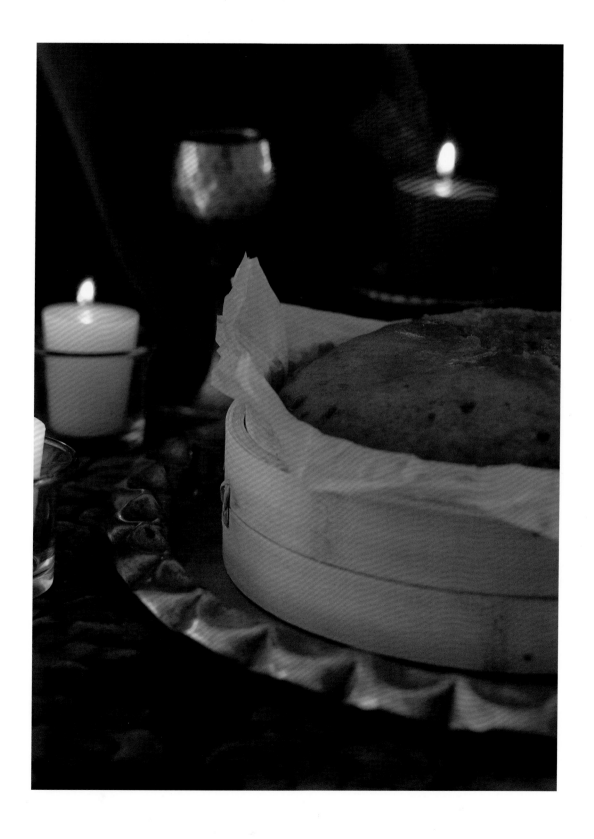

螢火蟲

ROLL & *SQUISH.*
YOU SQUASH
THEM WITH
YOUR THUMBS.
LIKE BUGS.

River

RIVER'S

HODGEBERRY THUMBPRINTS

24 COOKIES

TIME
Prep: 10 minutes
Bake: 15 minutes

COURSE
Sweet

DIETARY
Veg

DIFFICULTY
Easy

INGREDIENTS

1 stick butter
½ cup sugar
1 egg
Pinch of salt
1 tsp vanilla extract
1½ cups flour
½ cup jam, hodgeberry
or otherwise

METHOD

Preheat the oven to 350°F and line a baking sheet with parchment paper.

Cream together the butter and sugar until pale and fluffy, then add in the egg, salt, and vanilla. Mix in the flour until you get a nice soft dough. Form into 24 balls and place evenly on the prepared baking sheet. Using your thumb, press an indent into the top of each cookie. Fill each indent with about a teaspoon of jam. Bake for 15 minutes, until the bottoms of the cookies are golden brown. Eat them the same day.

螢火蟲

Five-Spice Caramel

THIS VERSATILE RECIPE MAKES RICHLY SPICED CARAMEL THAT CAN EITHER BE USED AS A SAUCE OR MADE INTO INDIVIDUAL CANDIES. ORIGINALLY MADE POPULAR IN THE BORDER PLANETS, WHERE SIMPLE INGREDIENTS COULD BE COMBINED FOR A RARE TREAT, IT HAS SINCE GAINED POPULARITY IN THE CORE WORLDS AS WELL, WHERE IT IS USED AS A DECADENT DRIZZLE OVER PRETENTIOUS DESSERTS.

MAKES: 1 DOZEN

COOK: 15 MIN

GF, VEG

CLASS: DESSERT

DIFFICULTY: MIDDLING

INGREDIENTS:
1 cup sugar
1 cup honey
8 tbsp butter
1 cup heavy cream
1 tsp vanilla
½ tsp salt
½ tsp five-spice mix

If you plan to make individual caramels, line an 8 inch x 8 inch square pan with lightly buttered parchment paper.

In a medium saucepan, combine the sugar, honey, and water. Bring up to a simmer and let cook until it darkens somewhat and reaches around 275ºF. Add the remaining ingredients, stirring briskly a few times, then replace on the heat. Cook until the mixture comes back up to a bubble. At this point, remove from heat if you'd like a caramel sauce, or continue to cook until it reaches 250ºF again for bite-sized caramels. Pour the hot caramel into the prepared pan and let cool for around an hour in the fridge. Once cool, pull the caramels from the pan using the parchment paper. Peel the paper off and place the caramel sheet on a cutting board. Using a buttered sharp knife, cut into small rectangles. Either enjoy immediately or wrap in individual candy papers to store.

MAL'S
ALMOND COOKIES
24 COOKIES

Almonds are costly to produce, making them the purview of the wealthy. Far as I'm concerned, rich folk can keep their fancy ingredients, but these here cookies? They're worth a bit of trouble. Might be I stuffed a few into my pockets last shindig I found myself attending, but I won't swear to it.

TIME
Prep: 10 minutes
Bake: 15 minutes

COURSE
Sweet

DIETARY
Veg

DIFFICULTY
Easy

INGREDIENTS

1 stick butter
½ cup sugar
1 eggs, plus one for wash
½ tsp almond extract
¼ cup almond flour
½ tsp baking soda
Pinch of salt
1½ cups flour
24 whole almonds

METHOD

Preheat your oven to 350°F and line a baking sheet with parchment paper.

In a medium mixing bowl, cream together the butter and sugar. Next, add the egg, almond extract, almond flour, soda, and salt. Finally, mix in the flour until you have a nice firm dough that ain't too sticky. Make the dough into 24 little balls and space 'em evenly on the baking sheet. Press an almond into the top of each one and brush with the last egg, beaten with a little water. Bake for about 15 minutes, until nice and golden colored.

螢火蟲

螢火蟲

INARA'S

SHIMMERWINE

4 SERVINGS

It seems that each fancy party in the Core features a more elaborate cocktail than the last. In fact, I think it is something of a sport to try to outdo one another. I prefer a more straightforward offering that can still be had nearly everywhere. Shimmerwine looks the part, with its swirls of shimmering gold, but doesn't muddle the mind overmuch.

TIME
Prep: 15 minutes

COURSE
Drink

DIETARY
GF, Veg, Vegan

DIFFICULTY
Easy

INGREDIENTS

¼ cup orange liqueur or water
¼ cup sugar
¼ tsp ground ginger
Dash of edible gold luster dust
Chilled champagne or
        other bubbly wine

METHOD

In a small saucepan over medium heat, combine the liqueur, sugar, and ground ginger. Stir occasionally until the sugar has dissolved, then remove from heat. Stir in the luster dust, just enough to give the syrup a good shimmer, then let the syrup cool.

When you are ready to serve, pour about 1 Tbsp of the syrup into the bottom of your glass. Top up with champagne and adjust the level of shimmer, if needed. Serve immediately, as the shimmer will settle over time.

螢火蟲

EVERYTHING'S SO FANCY, AND THERE'S SOME KIND OF HOT CHEESE OVER THERE.

Kaylee

KAYLEE'S
FRYE FIZZLER
1 SERVING

I had this drink at that fancy shindig on Persephone where me and the cap'n was fixing to meet up with a buyer. I liked this a lot better than the shimmerwine, so I traded one of the waiters for the know-how. I got a recipe, and he got advice on how to fix his granny's hover-lift hydraulics. The drink didn't have no name of its own so I gave it mine. I reckon it would be a perfect drink for a summer weddin'...

TIME
Prep: 5 minutes

COURSE
Drink

DIETARY
GF, Veg, Vegan

DIFFICULTY
Easy

INGREDIENTS

1 sugar cube
2–3 drops rose water
1 oz orange liqueur
4–6 oz Champagne
Orange slice and maraschino cherry,
to garnish

METHOD

Drop the sugar cube into the bottom of a champagne flute and add the rose water on top of it. Pour the orange liqueur on top of that and, finally, top up with champagne. Garnish and serve straight away.

螢火蟲

SIMON'S

GOLDEN MILK

1 SERVING

I remember my father used to drink a cup of this every night before bed. I tried it once in the kitchen, and thought it was just terrible. As I've gotten older, though, I better understand its health benefits. The warm milk relaxes the body for sleep, while the spices offer a wide range of healing properties. It's funny how only a snippet of a memory can stay with us — I can't see or smell turmeric without thinking of my father.

TIME
Prep: 10 minutes

COURSE
Drink

DIETARY
GF, Veg, Vegan*

DIFFICULTY
Easy

INGREDIENTS

1½ cups milk
1 cinnamon stick
½ tsp dried turmeric
1 tsp freshly grated ginger
1 Tbsp honey
1 tsp coconut oil
¼ tsp whole black peppercorns
Ground cinnamon (for serving)

METHOD

Combine all ingredients in a small saucepan over medium heat. Bring to a simmer, then reduce heat to medium-low for around 5–10 minutes to let the flavors steep. Strain into a heat-proof mug or teacup and serve hot, sprinkled with cinnamon.

螢火蟲

SAKE COCKTAIL

1 SERVING, PLUS EXTRA SYRUP

Enough years have gone by that I can just about drink this again. It used to be my favorite drink while I was in medical school on Osiris but, after an especially embarrassing incident after graduation involving a few too many of these and a rather large statue of Hippocrates... let's just say we had to part ways.

TIME
Syrup: 35 minutes
Prep: 5 minutes

COURSE
Drink

DIETARY
GF, Veg, Vegan

DIFFICULTY
Easy

INGREDIENTS	METHOD

SYRUP

½ cucumber, shredded
½ cup sugar
½ cup water
2 inches fresh ginger, sliced thin

COCKTAIL

2½ oz sake
½ oz melon liqueur
½ oz lime juice

Start off by making the simple syrup: combine the cucumber, sugar, water, and ginger in a small saucepan over medium heat. Cook just long enough for the sugar to dissolve, then remove from heat and let sit for around 30 minutes to let the flavors infuse. Strain into a clean bottle when cool.

To make the drink, add 1 oz of the simple syrup along with the other ingredients to a shaker filled with ice. Give it a few good shakes, then strain into a rocks glass with a few ice cubes in it.

螢火蟲

RECIPES FROM THE CORE WORLDS, UNDERBELLY

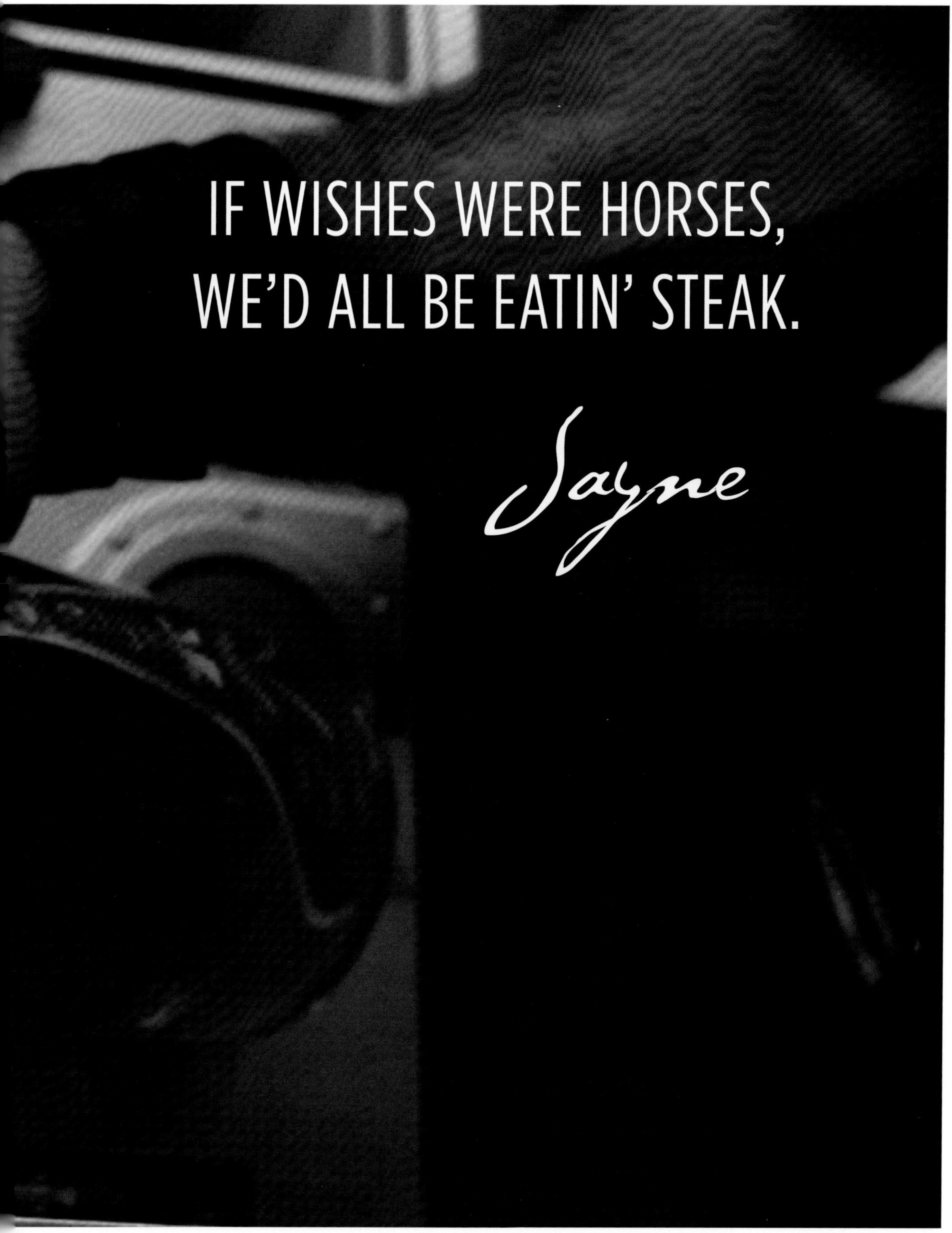

IF WISHES WERE HORSES,
WE'D ALL BE EATIN' STEAK.

Jayne

FINGER ... HES

The thing you gotta understa... ...s like you do.
Appearance is everything, savvy? ...vincing, I serves
them a little tea, maybe some d... ...e yet. And if it
does, well..

TIME
Prep: 10 minutes

COURSE
Snack

DIETARY
GF*, Veg

DIFFICULTY
Easy

INGREDIENTS

6 slices wheat bread, lightly toasted
7 oz cream cheese
1 cucumber, sliced thin
6 slices cheddar cheese
1 apple, cored and sliced thin
2 Tbsp lemon juice

METHOD

Set out your slices of bread and spread them all with a layer of cream cheese. Pile a layer of cucumber on three of the pieces of bread, then a slice of cheddar. Toss the apple slices with the lemon juice to prevent them browning, then layer those on top of the cheese. Add the rest of the cheddar on top of the apple slices, then flip an empty slice of bread onto the top of each sandwich. Trim the crusts off with a sharp knife, then cut into triangles. Serve on a nice china plate.

螢火蟲

WASH'S

SPICED TEA EGGS

6 EGGS

I love these eggs. Not as much as I love my wife, because she is the best wife, of all the wives. But these are the best eggs. You can usually find them being made in the market districts of the big cities, in these huge steaming pots. They're flavorful and spiced, but portable, which makes them great snacks for while you collect all the necessary goods for the ship.

TIME
Prep: 20 minutes
Soak: 12–24 hrs

COURSE
Snack

DIETARY
GF, Veg

DIFFICULTY
Middling

INGREDIENTS	METHOD

INGREDIENTS

6 eggs
4 Tbsp soy sauce
½ tsp Sichuan peppercorns
1 star anise
1 cinnamon stick
2 tsp sugar
½ tsp salt
2 black tea bags
2½ cups water, plus more as needed

METHOD

Boil the eggs in enough water to cover them for about 10 minutes, then drain and run under cold water until cool enough to handle. Gently crack the eggs all over but do not peel, then move them to a small bowl and set aside.

Combine the remaining ingredients in a small saucepan over medium heat. Cover and bring up to a simmer, then cook for about 10 minutes.

Discard the tea bags and pour the liquid over the bowl of eggs, then add as much water as needed to cover the eggs. Place in the fridge and let soak for 12–24 hours, depending on the strength of flavor you like.

JAYNE'S
SAUSAGE ROLLS
10 SERVINGS

Kaylee said I didn't write enough in my other recipes. What d'ya want me to say? It's food, you eat it. These is served all over the 'Verse, mostly in the disreputable parts of cities. My kinda places. They're real good so long as you don't look too close at what's in it. Kinda like everything in them city blocks.

TIME
Prep: 5 minutes
Rise: 20 minutes
Steam: 30 minutes

COURSE
Savory

DIETARY
N/A

DIFFICULTY
Middling

INGREDIENTS

1 batch of bao dough, page 20
10 Chinese sausages
10 pieces of parchment paper,
cut into 3 x 4 inch
rectangles

METHOD

Prepare your bao dough just as it says on page 20, and let it rise. Put your sausages on a plate in a steamer basket set over a pan of simmering water, and steam 'em for 10 minutes. Take the steamer off the heat.

When the dough has risen, punch it down and divide into 10 pieces. Roll each piece of dough into a rope about 12 inches long, then wrap the dough around the sausage. Put the wrapped sausage on a piece of paper, then put them in the steamer tray, off the heat, to rise for 20 minutes. Move the steamer to the stove and steam for about 15 minutes, until they're all puffy. Eat 'em warm, or stick 'em on skewers for walkin' around with.

螢火蟲

螢火蟲

MEAT PIES

6 LARGE HAND PIES

I ate one of these on Persephone. Then I ate another and another and then Simon made me stop.
He said I'd be sick. He's stupid.

Thank you, River. That's a very intelligent contribution.

TIME

Prep: 30 minutes
Cook: 40 minutes

COURSE

Main

DIETARY

N/A

DIFFICULTY

Middling

INGREDIENTS

1 Tbsp sesame oil

1–2 cloves garlic, minced

1 Tbsp minced ginger

1 onion, diced

1 medium carrot, minced

1 lb ground beef

1 Tbsp rice wine

3 Tbsp soy sauce

¼ tsp freshly ground Sichuan
      pepper, or black pepper

½ tsp fennel seeds,
      ground

1 tsp salt

2 Tbsp brown sugar

2 batches chilled pastry dough,
      page 20

1 egg for glaze, beaten

METHOD

Preheat the oven to 350°F and line a baking sheet or two with parchment paper. Heat the sesame oil in a frying pan over medium heat. Add the garlic and ginger and cook for a minute or so, until soft and fragrant. Add the onion and carrot and cook for another minute or so, then stir in the beef. Cook the beef until browned, a few minutes. Add the rice wine, 2 Tbsp soy sauce, the pepper, fennel, salt, and brown sugar. Stir everything together, then remove from heat and let cool for at least 15 minutes.

When you are ready to assemble the pies, divide the pastry dough into 6 equal balls. Roll a ball of dough into a flat disc, then heap ⅙ of the filling onto half the disc. Fold the dough over the top of the filling and crimp with a fork. Repeat for all the pies, placing each on the baking sheets. Beat the remaining tablespoon of soy sauce with the egg, then brush it onto the sealed pies. Bake for 40 minutes, until dark brown and sizzling.

Every city has its own variation of street skewers.

Skewers can be grilled, baked, or broiled.

THE IMPORTANT THING IS THE SPICES.
A MAN CAN LIVE ON PACKAGED FOOD
FROM HERE 'TIL JUDGMENT DAY IF
HE'S GOT ENOUGH ROSEMARY.

Book

BOOK'S

STREET CHICKEN
SKEWERS

4 - 6 SKEWERS

When I was young, it was mostly the affordability of street chicken that appealed but, as I grew and saw more of the world, I began to love them for their adaptability. Every city has its own variation, it seems, and I've seen versions with fiery pepper sauce, creamy peanut sauce, and everything in between. Even now, when I visit a new place, I make a point to try the local street chicken recipe.

TIME
Prep: 5 minutes
Marinate: 2+ hours
Cook: 15–20 minutes

COURSE
Savory

DIETARY
GF

DIFFICULTY
Middling

INGREDIENTS

2 boneless chicken thighs, cubed
1 Tbsp five-spice mix
¾ cup water
½ cup brown sugar
¼ cup soy sauce
2 Tbsp vegetable oil
3 cloves garlic, minced
1 Tbsp cornstarch
½ tsp paprika or spicy pepper

METHOD

In a small bowl, combine all the ingredients except the cornstarch and paprika. Cover and let marinate at least 2 hours. At the same time, submerge several bamboo skewers in water to soak.

When you are ready to cook, preheat the oven to 450°F and set out a baking sheet. Thread the pieces of chicken onto the soaked bamboo skewers and set on the baking sheet. Reserve the marinade. Bake for around 15–20 minutes, depending on the size of your chicken.

While the chicken is cooking, pour the marinade liquid into a pan, bring up to a simmer over medium heat, and cook for around 5 minutes. In a separate small bowl, combine the cornstarch with a splash of cold water, stirring until dissolved. Add the cornstarch solution to the saucepan and cook, stirring, for another minute or two, until combined and thick. Remove from heat. When the chicken skewers are finished cooking, either dip them in the sauce or brush the sauce onto the skewers. Sprinkle with paprika and serve hot.

TIP: The skewers can also be grilled with great success, for just a couple of minutes on each side, until cooked through.

RIVER'S
CANDIED
FRUIT SKEWERS
6 - 10 SKEWERS

Crunchy fruit. Daddy bought them for me on the street. Like jewels in the window of a jeweler's shop, all glittery and vivid. Strawberries like blood.

TIME
Prep: 30 minutes

COURSE
Sweet

DIETARY
GF, Veg, Vegan

DIFFICULTY
Complex

INGREDIENTS

2 cups granulated sugar
½ cup light corn syrup
1 cup water
1 pound fresh fruits
Bamboo skewers

METHOD

Combine the sugar, corn syrup, and water in a small saucepan over medium heat; don't stir it. Set a baking sheet nearby with a silicone liner on it (aluminum foil or parchment paper brushed lightly with oil will also work). Set a large bowl of ice water nearby as well.

Thread the fruits onto the skewers, a few on each, in pretty patterns. When the sugar syrup reaches 300°F, take it off the heat and dip the bottom of the saucepan into the bowl of ice water, making sure no water spills into the syrup. When the syrup stops bubbling, take it out of the ice bath. Working quickly, tilt the pan so the syrup gathers, then dip in a skewer of fruit, turning so the syrup covers the fruit completely. Let the excess drip off, then place the skewer on the prepared baking sheet. Let the skewers cool completely before eating.

螢火蟲

螢火蟲

YOUTIAO - FRIED CRULLERS

8 - 10 YOUTIAO

Oh gosh, I just love these fried dough sticks! If you can find 'em being made fresh, that's the best way, so's they come out of the oil all hot and bubbling. Then you bite one and it's crunchy on the outside, but then soft and chewy on the inside. They're real popular street foods on some of the Core worlds, but on our side of town, not the fancy parts.

螢火蟲

TIME

Dough Prep: 5 minutes
Rest: 12 hours
Fry: 20 minutes

COURSE

Sweet

DIETARY

Veg

DIFFICULTY

Complex

INGREDIENTS

2 cups all-purpose flour
½ tsp salt
1 ½ tsp baking powder
1 egg
1 Tbsp milk
2 Tbsp butter, softened
⅓ cup water
Oil, for frying

METHOD

Combine the flour, salt, baking powder, egg, milk, and butter together in a large mixing bowl. Mix in just enough water to bring the dough together without it gettin' sticky. Now this is the tough part: you gotta knead it for ten minutes, or it won't be fluffy enough. It should be real soft, but not sticky. When you get it there, make it into a long rectangular shape, about 4 inches wide and ¼ inch thick. Wrap it in plastic and put in the fridge overnight.

The next day, take the dough out and let it warm up for a couple hours. Heat up the oil in a big pan over medium heat to about 400°F. Unwrap the dough and chop it width-wise into strips about 1 x 4 inches. Stack the strips in pairs, then dip a chopstick in flour and press it lengthwise down the middle of the stacked dough. Press down real hard to kinda squish 'em together to make an X shape cross-section. Then stretch the dough a little to make the strip longer, maybe 8 inches long. Drop the dough into the hot oil, and it should pop back up to the top. Use tongs or some old chop-sticks and keep the dough turning so it browns on all sides. Should take maybe a minute to cook, then you gotta scoop it out onto a plate lined with paper towels to drain.

I like 'em with some powdered sugar and cinnamon on top, but if you've got a can of condensed milk, you can dip 'em in and it's real good that way. Or try 'em with the caramel sauce from page 116.

Li Shen's Bazaar serves the best Ice Planets in the 'Verse, in many different flavours.

Ice Planets are made up of three layers — the core, mantle, and crust.

MY FOOD IS PROBLEMATIC.

River

ICE PLANETS

4 SERVINGS

This is not a moon. Neither is it a planet, although the layers are similar to stellar bodies orbiting suns.
VERY PROBLEMATIC.

TIME
Core: 20+ minutes
Mantle: 15 minutes
Crust: 10 minutes

COURSE
Sweet

DIETARY
GF, Veg*

DIFFICULTY
Problematic

INGREDIENTS

CORE

10 oz bag chocolate chips
⅔ cup heavy cream
4 Tbsp cocoa powder
1 tsp ground ginger
4 pieces of string (2 feet long)
4 dowels

MANTLE

5 Tbsp butter
½ cups peanut butter
1 Tbsp honey
10 oz bag marshmallows
6 cups puffed rice cereal

CRUST

12 oz white chocolate chips
        or baking chocolate
3 oz coconut oil
Pinch of salt

METHOD - CORE

Pour the chocolate chips into a small bowl. In a small saucepan, mix together the heavy cream, cocoa powder, and ginger. Bring to a simmer then pour the cream mixture over the chocolate chips. Stir until the chocolate has melted and the mixture is completely smooth, then chill for 1–2 hours.

Once the chocolate mixture is cool, scoop out roughly 2 Tbsp at a time and form into a ball around a piece of string, leaving about 4 inches hanging out one side. Place in the fridge to cool. Once chilled, trim off any excess string. You'll only need 4 cores on string, so the rest of the mixture can be made into individual truffles.

TIP: Many people have varying opinions on how an Ice Planet ought to be eaten. Some argue it's meant to be cut open to expose the layers, while others favor winding the string up the dowel to stabilize it enough to take a bite. Whatever your method, hands-free is best to keep the chocolate from melting.

METHOD - MANTLE

Combine the butter, peanut butter, and honey in a large saucepan over medium-low heat, and stir until completely melted. Add the marshmallows, and stir for around 10 minutes, until they are melted and entirely incorporated. Remove from the heat and stir in the rice cereal. Turn the mixture out onto a silicone mat or a buttered surface to cool down. When it is cool enough to handle, butter your hands to keep them from sticking and scoop up ¼ of the mix. Press this around one of the chilled chocolate truffle cores until you've formed a smooth ball and the chocolate core is completely enclosed. Return to the fridge to chill.

METHOD - CRUST

Combine the ingredients in a medium mixing bowl, then microwave in short bursts until completely melted and smooth. Let cool to room temperature. Working with one chilled ice planet at a time, dip into the chocolate and roll until completely coated. Let any excess drip off, then place on a plate. Tie the loose end of string to a dowel and you're ready to enjoy!

WASH'S
BLUE HURRICANE
1 SERVING

There's this terrific little dive on Persephone, and I mean really terrible, with dim lights, very sticky floors, the works. But they serve great drinks, and I always try to stop in if we are there long enough. Despite the overall thuggery of their usual clientele, they have a robust selection of tropical drinks. You know, the ones with the little umbrellas? I love the little umbrellas.

TIME
Prep: 5 minutes

COURSE
Drink

DIETARY
GF, Veg, Vegan

DIFFICULTY
Easy

INGREDIENTS

1 oz Rum
1 oz Blue Curacao or Schnapps
2 oz pineapple juice
1 oz orange juice
Citrus for garnish
Ice, crushed

METHOD

Fill a tall glass half full with ice, then pour the ingredients over. Garnish with some fruit, and at least one little umbrella. Maybe two.

螢火蟲

ZOE'S
GUNPOWDER GIMLET
1 SERVING, PLUS EXTRA SYRUP

You can get versions of this at any number of bars throughout the 'Verse, but the best I ever had was on Gonghe before the war. I don't know if that bar is even still standing, or what they did to make the drink so good but, near as I can tell, this is the basic recipe.

TIME
Tea Syrup: 15 minutes
Prep: 5 minutes

COURSE
Drink

DIETARY
GF, Veg, Vegan

DIFFICULTY
Middling

INGREDIENTS

GREEN TEA SYRUP

1 cup water
1 cup sugar
1 cup loose gunpowder green tea

GUNPOWDER GIMLET

1½ oz gin
1 oz tea syrup (above)
Dash fresh lime juice
2 oz club soda
Lemon slices and mint for garnish
Ice

METHOD

GREEN TEA SYRUP

Combine the water and sugar in a small saucepan over medium heat and cook until the sugar has dissolved. Remove from the heat.

Pour the loose tea into a large jar or bowl, then pour the hot sugar solution over it. Let steep for about 5 minutes, then strain into a clean container. Keep chilled for up to a week.

GUNPOWDER GIMLET

Combine the gin, tea syrup, and lime juice in a shaker half filled with ice. Give it a few good shakes, then strain into a lowball glass. Add an ice cube or two, then top up with club soda. Garnish and serve, quick as that.

RECIPES BY COURSE

INDEX

THE BASICS 14

 ## SNACKS

 ## SAVORY

SWEET

 ## DRINK

DIETARY INFORMATION

RECIPE	GLUTEN FREE	VEGETARIAN	VEGAN
Almond Cookies		x	
Bacon & Cheese Toast	x*		
Badger's Finger Sandwiches	x*	x	
Biscuits		x	x†
Blue Hurricane	x	x	x
Border Berry Cordial	x	x	x
Bread Pudding		x	
Brown Sauce	x	x*	x*
Canapes – Stuffed Mushrooms		x	x*
Canapes – Sweet Potato Bites	x	x	x
Canapes – Tofu Cubes	x	x	
Candied Fruit Skewers	x	x	x
Canned Peach Cobbler		x	
Cheesy Grits	x	x	
Chicken & Dumplings			
Chocolate Protein Cake		x	
Companion Tea	x	x	x
Corn Dodgers	x	x*	x*
Crab Dip	x		
Crunchy Snack Mix	x*	x	x*
Dough for Bao		x	x
Dried Spiro-balls	x	x	x
Eggy Oat Mush	x	x	
Family Soup	x		
Five-spice Caramel	x	x	
Fresh Bao		x	x
Fresh Tomato Slices	x	x	x
Fruit Oaty Bars		x	x*
Frye Fizzler	x	x	x
Garlic Green Beans	x	x	x
Garlic Griddle Bread		x*	
Ginger Spiced Steamer Cake		x	
Goat Curry	x		
Golden Milk	x	x	x*
Gunpowder Gimlet	x	x	x
Haymaker's Punch	x	x	x

	GLUTEN FREE	VEGETARIAN	VEGAN
Hodgeberry Thumbprints		x	
Ice Planets	x	x*	
Lotus Chips	x	x	x
Mama Reynolds' Shoofly Pie		x	
Mandarin Salad	x	x	x*
Mashed Sesame Spuds	x	x	x*
Matcha Macaron Drops	x	x	
Meat Pies			
Molasses Taffy Twists	x	x	x*
Mudder's Milk	x	x	
Mulled Wine	x	x	x
Pastry Dough		x*	x*
Pork & Beans	x		
Pork Hash	x		
Pork Jerky	x		
Roast Duck	x		
Saffron Rice Pudding	x	x	x*
Sake Cocktail	x	x	x
Sausage Rolls			
Shadow Spare Ribs	x		
Shepherd Chicken Soup	x*		
Shimmerwine	x	x	x
Shipboard Crackers		x	x
Southdown Abbey Couscous with Roasted Vegetables		x	x*
Spaghetti Casserole	x*		
Spiced Lamb	x		
Spiced Plum Fruit Leather	x	x	x
Spiced Tea Eggs	x	x	
Steamed Pumpkin Buns		x	x
Strawberry Shortcake		x	
Street Chicken Skewers	x		
Sweet Chili Sauce	x	x	x
Tear & Share Rolls		x	
White Sauce		x	x*
Wife Soup	x	x	x*
Youtiao - Fried Crullers		x	

CULINARY CONVERSION

VOLUME

IMPERIAL	CUPS	METRIC
-	¼ tsp	1.25 ml
-	½ tsp	2.5 ml
-	1 tsp	5 ml
-	1 tbsp	15 ml
3 ½ fl oz	-	100 ml
4 ½ fl oz	½ cup	125 ml
5 fl oz	-	150 ml
7 fl oz	-	200 ml
9 fl oz	1 cup	250 ml
11 fl oz	-	300 ml
14 fl oz	-	400 ml
18 fl oz	2 cups	500 ml
26 fl oz	3 cups	750 ml
35 fl oz	4 cups	1L
53 fl oz	6 cups	1.5L
70 fl oz	8 cups	2L

WEIGHT

IMPERIAL	METRIC
½ oz	15g
1 oz	30g
2 oz	60g
3 oz	85g
4 oz (¼lb)	115g
5 oz	140g
6 oz	170g
7 oz	200g
8 oz (½lb)	230g
16 oz (1lb)	450g
32 oz (2 lb)	950g
35 oz (2 ⅕ lb)	1kg

TEMPERATURE

FAHRENHEIT	CELSIUS	GAS
250°F	120°C	½
275°F	140°C	1
300°F	150°C	2
325°F	160°C	3
350°F	180°C	4
375°F	190°C	5
400°F	200°C	6
425°F	220°C	7
450°F	230°C	8
475°F	240°C	9
500°F	260°C	10

LENGTH

IMPERIAL	METRIC
¼ in	6mm
½ in	13mm
1 in	25mm
2 in	51mm
1 ft	305mm
1 ft 8 in	500mm
1 yard	915mm
3 ft 3 in	1000mm
70 fl oz	8 cups

For Corey, whose help was invaluable, and
Jocelyn (Ma Schreiber), who helped make
Canton a little more real.

And for Brent, for always.